From BROKENNESS *To* BRILLIANCE:

Finding Purpose and Passion in Your Pain

From Brokenness to Brilliance: Finding Purpose and Passion in Your Pain
Copyright © 2025 by Dr. Lashonda Wofford.
All Rights Reserved

No part of this book may be used or reproduced in any manner whatsoever without written permission from the publisher, except in the case of brief quotations embodied in critical articles and reviews. For permissions, inquiries, or additional information, please contact the publisher via:

All Bets On Me | Dr. Lashonda Wofford
Email: **info@drlashondawofford.com**
Website: **www.drlashondawofford.com**

Cover Design: Xee Shan
Images Provided By: Dr. Lashonda Wofford and contributing authors.

All scripture quotations are taken from
The Holy Bible, King James Version (KJV) – Public Domain.
First Edition

ISBNs:
Paperback: 979-8-9923605-0-9
eBook: 979-8-9923605-1-6

Printed in the United States of America

Disclaimer: The stories, testimonies, and reflections shared in this book are based on personal experiences. While every effort has been made to ensure accuracy, this book is not intended as a substitute for professional advice, counseling, or therapy.

Dedication

To every woman who has ever walked through the fire of pain, loss, and adversity yet still found the courage to rise—this book is for you.

To the warriors who have fought silent battles, the overcomers who have transformed their wounds into wisdom, and the resilient souls who have turned their pain into purpose—your story matters.

I dedicate this book to my beloved grandmother Mildred Brewington and my aunts Geraldine Brewington, Gladys Miller and Gloria Alston, whose love and legacy continue to inspire me every day. Your memory fuels my purpose, and your presence is forever imprinted on my heart.

To my family, friends, and sisterhood of purpose-driven women—your unwavering support, prayers, and encouragement have been my anchor.

And to the eight phenomenal women who bravely share their journeys in this book—thank you for standing in your truth, for being a light to others, and for proving that from brokenness comes brilliance.

May this book be a testament that no matter how deep the pain, God has a plan for restoration, renewal, and radiant purpose.

With love and gratitude,

Dr. Lashonda Wofford
Visionary Author

DR. LASHONDA WOFFORD
Visionary Author

Acknowledgments

With a heart full of gratitude, I extend my deepest appreciation to everyone who made this book possible. This journey has been one of faith, resilience, and purpose, and I am honored to share it with the world alongside these incredible women.

First and foremost, I give all glory and honor to God. Through every challenge, every tear, and every moment of doubt, He has been my source of strength, my anchor, and my guiding light. Without His grace, this book—and my journey—would not be possible.

To the nine phenomenal women who courageously share their stories in these pages—thank you for your transparency, your strength, and your willingness to empower others through your truth. Your voices matter, and your testimonies will inspire countless lives.

To my family—your unwavering love and support have carried me through my toughest moments. Thank you for believing in me, praying for me, and standing by my side as I continue to walk in my purpose.

To my sisterhood of friends, colleagues, and mentors—your encouragement, wisdom, and affirmations have lifted me higher than I could have imagined. Your presence in my life reminds me that no one succeeds alone.

To my dear readers—whether you are in the midst of your storm or have already emerged stronger—know that you are not alone. Your pain has a purpose, and your story is still being written. My prayer is that these pages bring you hope, healing, and the courage to rise beyond your trials.

Finally, to every person who believed in this vision, supported this project, or simply spoke life into me when I needed it most—thank you. This book is more than a collection of stories; it is a movement of resilience, empowerment, and divine transformation.

May *From Brokenness to Brilliance* serve as a beacon of hope, reminding us all that from every trial, God can birth something powerful, beautiful, and purposeful.

With love and gratitude,
Dr. Lashonda Wofford
Visionary Author

Table of Content

Foreword..ix
Introduction..xvii

CHAPTER 1: THE BREAKING POINT 1
When Everything Changes by Marcy Jessup

CHAPTER 2: IN THE DEPTHS OF DESPAIR: 18
Coping in the Seasons of Darkness by Pastor Yolanda Pinkney-Coleman

CHAPTER 3: FROM BROKENNESS TO BRILLIANCE: 38
Finding Purpose and Passion Beyond Your Pain by Sandra Wolf

CHAPTER 4: BEYOND THE VERDICT: 52
A Journey from Pain to Power by Dr. Iris Wright

CHAPTER 5: TURNING PAIN INTO PURPOSE : 64
Peace over panic, Faith over Fear, Wisdom Over Worry! by Dawanna Alexander

CHAPTER 6: CULTIVATING PASSION AND CONFIDENCE:..81
Rebuilding Self-Esteem and Rediscovering Joy by Dr. Karon Graves

CHAPTER 7: FROM SILENCE TO SIGNIFICANCE:................102
Reclaiming My Voice, Boldness, and Brilliance by Carol Andrews King

CHAPTER 8: FROM BROKENNESS TO BRILLIANCE: 119
The Power of Community and Walking in Purpose by Dr. Lashonda Wofford

WORKBOOK & GUIDED JOURNAL 140

Foreword

By Dr Jacquelyn Wilson

" Life is not about how short we fall, it's about how tall we stand in our beliefs after tripping." - The Street Doctor

If you are reading this, know that YOU'RE HERE FOR A REASON. This date, this time, this particular book in your hands—it's all a part of God's divine timing. Everything you've gone through, good or bad, was all designed for His will for your life.

Life has a way of teaching us, sometimes breaking us in ways we never imagined. For me, the years 2018 and 2023 were marked by unimaginable loss—first, the passing of my significant other of 14 years. One moment, our relationship was clinging by a thread, and the next moment, he was clinging to life. Then, just when I thought I had found my footing, eight more loved ones were taken in a single year. My mom passed away on December 1st, 2022, and it felt as if she was taking everyone with her.

I began losing my pillars one by one—all winter, spring, summer, and fall. I had never experienced anything like this in my life. After the 6th death, my brother died on 8/28/23. He suffered a heart attack in Riverside Park in Harlem.

As fate would have it, I lost my sister the morning of his funeral, September 12th, 2023. It was the first time I felt my heart shatter. Death visited me. Grief became my constant companion, and for a time, I lived in the shadows of pain, wondering if I would ever emerge whole again.

Then, I began reading my sister's articles. Ruthe McDonald was a published author, journalist, editor, and a prolific writer. Her last article, titled "GONE," was published in August 2023. She knew she was dying. She left a detailed to-do list on how to overcome grief, pain, and sudden loss. She loved God and professed how nothing and no one was more important than our relationship with him. She emphasized that people could perish at any moment, but what mattered was how solid our faith in Him is.

Somehow, she coached me out of my pain. I asked myself, "Why not me?" I felt blessed to have been chosen to endure such a profound responsibility. "God, you trust me? With all of this?" I said, "Wow, you've got jokes!"

Through every tear, every dark night, and every moment I felt like giving up, I discovered a deeper strength within me—a brilliance that had been there all along, waiting to shine.

We cannot experience breakthroughs without breaking. As I mend myself on a daily via teaching, coaching, motivational speaking, and facilitating the youth in detention centers, I've unlocked a new level of purpose!

One thing is for certain, and two things are for sure: I'm no stranger to struggle, homelessness, teen pregnancy, and grieving the dead or living. I was forced to let some people go. I've learned we cannot love the red flags out of people!

This book is for anyone who has ever felt lost in grief, anyone who has questioned whether joy could ever return, and anyone who is searching for the light at the end of their darkest tunnel. I invite you to walk with me through my journey from pain to pages, brokenness to brilliance. May my testimony remind you that even in our deepest sorrows, we are never truly alone. God is with you every step of the way. Grief may be a lonely road; however, death is a life teacher. Keep sparkling, gem. Let nothing stop you, and if you ever come to a halt, dig deeper; there's more to you!

DR JACQUELYN WILSON
Aka The Streetdoctor

Dr. Jacquelyn Wilson chaplain is on a mission. From Award-winning Motivational Keynote Speaker to Celebrity Coach, Executive Director and Celebrity Host, the Dr. is a formidable force inspiring the world. As CEO of Mynding My Own Bizness® Entertainment, she executive produced the three-time, award-winning short film, The Bully, winner of HBO presents, for its powerful message against bullying and intolerance. The movie led to the development of The Stop Bullying Project®.

Dr. Wilson is the Founder and Executive Director of #SurpriseTheStruggling™ Inc., a global hashtag movement and Non-Profit Organization with international connections. Dr. Wilson assists women and teen girls through the transitions of homelessness, surprising women with purses filled with toiletries and other necessary hygienic items.

In conjunction with The Doctor Wilson Leadership Academy, #SurpriseTheStruggling™ also provides monthly Tea Huddles for women in transition, offering them a place to regroup and gain resources on what they need to move forward in their lives. The Tea Huddles are a national program taking place in various cities across the United States.

Dr. Wilson also hosts a Grief Circle for women & men assisting them as they grapple with the pain of losing a loved one.

The DWLA also facilitates a (Clarity Coaching) workshop for less fortunate beginner entrepreneurs "In the community" twice a month at the Staten Island mall, in the emblem health space.

Dr. Wilson is also a proud member of the National Council Of Negro Women Staten Island chapter , and an active ODAEP Social Emotional Learning Teaching Expert Instructor /mentor.

As board Treasurer Of Harlem Nyc #1 Anti Gun Violence Organization Street Corner Resources, she stays connected with her community, evoking change De escalating violence, providing opportunities ensuring the safety of our youth via music studios, recording, anti bullying workshops, poetry, open mics and, the PEACE cafe with Dr. Iesha Sekou!

She is also the Founder of Queen's Don't Trip We Adjust Our Crowns And Aim, a monthly educational trip to the gun range to teach women on how to become licensed to carry legally! Dr. Wilson exemplifies advocacy and strategic planning in her ability to not only see the need, but also develop sustainable programming to alleviate community issues.

Dr. Wilson has received numerous accolades and awards for her philanthropic/humanitarian work in the community. She is the recipient of 12 NYS Citations.

- 2024 Achi Mag Positive Social Influencer
- 2023 NYC Council Unsung Hero Honoree
- 2023 I Am Woman Honoree
- 2023 Breathe Again Champion for Change
- 2023 Phenomenal Woman Honoree
- 2022 Achi Mag Master Coach of The Year

- 2022 Public Advocate Honoree
- 2022 Minority Woman in Biz Honoree
- 2022 JCP Plug of The Year Recipient
- 2022 Project Rehab Honoree
- 2021 Triumphant Speaker of The Year
- 2021 L'Oréal's Woman of Worth finalist
- 2020 Global Woman of Influence

She is also a:

- 5X Best Selling Author 4 Categories
- Co-Author of Sister's Inspiring Sisters
- Co-Author of Hartford's Litt Anthology
- Host of (Uncut Jewels) Podcast. Available on YouTube!
- Self-Published author of Noon Jewels Pieces of me VOL1 and Creator of Noonjewels Inspirational Apparel line . Both available at www.Noonjewels.com

For bookings:
- Email via: Dr.Wilson@Noonjeweles.com
- Visit www.Drjacquelynwilson.com, or
- www.Surprisethestruggling.org

You can also reach out via:
- Instagram.com/noonjewels_
- Facebook.com/Dr.Wilson
- https://youtube.com/shorts/BYKM0QjZ7sI

Introduction

There is something profoundly beautiful about a woman who has walked through the fire and weathered the storms yet still stands radiant, resilient, and unwavering in her faith. *From Brokenness to Brilliance: Finding Purpose and Passion in Your Pain* is not just a book; it is a divine testament to the extraordinary power of God to transform our deepest wounds into our greatest victories.

This powerful collection, written by women of faith, courage, strength, and resilience, is a beacon of hope for anyone who has ever felt crushed beneath the weight of life's hardships. We are women who have faced raging storms, endured the darkest nights, and journeyed through the valleys of pain that threatened to consume us. Yet, through it all, we discovered that brokenness is not the end of our story—it is the very place where God's hand is at work, shaping us, molding us, and birthing something extraordinary within us.

With every trial, setback, and moment of despair, we learned that pain is not just something to endure—it is a path to purpose. It is in the moments when we thought we were at our weakest that God revealed His greatest strength. It was in the tears we cried alone that

He whispered His promises of restoration. It was in the seasons of uncertainty that He planted seeds of purpose, showing us that every storm carries within it the potential for a breakthrough.

Now, we rise—not just as survivors but as warriors of faith, as women who have found purpose in the very things that once sought to break us. We stand as living proof that no matter how dark the road, how heavy the burden, or how painful the past is, there is *glory on the other side of pain.*

From Brokenness to Brilliance is more than a collection of stories; it is a movement. It is an anthem of victory for every woman who has ever felt unseen, unheard, or unworthy. Through these pages, you will find encouragement, empowerment, and the undeniable truth that your pain does not define you—your purpose does.

As you read the journeys of these incredible women, may you be inspired to embrace your own story, find strength in your struggles, and step boldly into the brilliance that awaits you because no matter where you've been or what you've endured, your story is still being written, and something *extraordinary* is on the other side.

Welcome to a journey of healing, hope, and purpose. Welcome to *From Brokenness to Brilliance.*

DR. LASHONDA WOFFORD
Visionary Author

CHAPTER 1
THE BREAKING POINT
When Everything Changes

By Marcy Jessup

"Don't Be Afraid To Be The Person God Called You To Be"

Little did I know that my journey, designed by the Creator and tailor-made just for me, would lead me to become who God has created me to be from the foundations of the world. Because He knew me before I was conceived in my mother's womb, He had a plan to unveil the gifts and talents He had hidden within me and use them to build people and for His glory.

This journey towards discovering who I am has been filled with many painful and hurtful moments and seasons of my life. Yet, it has also meant that I have had to first come to know the God that I serve, His mighty power, His love for me, and so much more. The great thing is that whatever I needed at any given time, all I had to do was access it from heaven.

This is how I was able to praise and worship Him simultaneously! I learned something about the power of worship earlier on in my journey. I now know it has been my weapon that made me resilient.

Testimony!!

Once I gave my life to Jesus, I was all in. I have always hungered for more and more of Him. My relationship with Jesus was first as a friend. I didn't know Him as a healer, a waymaker, a lawyer, or a promise keeper at the time. When I met Him, He was my best friend and still is to this day. I understood that I could share my thoughts with Him, that I could be myself, that I could unload all of my fears on Him, and that I could tell Him everything, and that is exactly what I did.

I am a person who needs to release my thoughts out loud! I loved my conversations with Jesus, my friend. I understood that I could express myself in the way that I felt them, and He would not judge me. Because Jesus knew me from the foundations of the world, nothing I said took him by surprise. When I think of some of the things that I said to him in prayer, it makes me smile. Being a babe in Christ with no known restrictions was liberating for me.

Again, this is part of my discovery of who Jesus is and also part of my self-discovery of who I am. This process will continue as long as I live.

I continued to grow in my faith in God, and as I encountered new devils at each level, I stayed true to God's word. I walked in love and continued to praise and worship God. I continued to fight with my weapons of praise, worship, and prayer.

As I look back over my journey of discovery, I now understand that God gave me a formula and a strategy for thriving. I am victorious! I win! He taught me the need to read His word, get grounded in His word, and walk in His love, even when loving like Jesus was, at times, very challenging for me.

The journey came with many tests and trials that I had to overcome. There were times when I didn't comprehend what and why I was being tested so often.

God taught me that praise and worship give me access to Him. When I was in that place in Him, I could ask for anything according to His will for my life, and He would answer. As a child of God, there is no place I would rather be than in His presence. It is in this place that His voice becomes so clear. It is in this place that He gives instructions for your life. It is in this place, the worship experience, that I became more aware of who I am and who I am not.

I am drawn to this place because I know that is where He is calling me. He is calling me into a higher place in Him. I learned that I am a warrior! I learned that when I am put to the test and the devil uses circumstances to come against me, I could use my weapons of praise and worship along with prayer.

As the journey continued, I realized that God had given me a strategy for my life in Him. If I implemented the strategy, I would have peace of mind, and even though the struggles and challenges were real, I would have the security of knowing that God was always with me.

What He gave me is the opportunity to live a lifestyle of praise and worship, stand on His word, and use prayer to push me forward. This is what my life has looked like on this journey of discovery.

As I moved into new areas of ministry, I had no idea of what to expect. What did I expect? One thing is that I expected it to look like someone else's ministry. The mistake that I made was not considering and praying about how this new area of ministry would look for me. I was naive. I had no mentors at all, no one to advise me on what my new role in ministry entailed. What was expected of me?

What I did have was the joy of the lord.

What I did have was faith in God.

What I did have was a servant's heart.

I walked into this new area of ministry expecting God to do great and mighty things. I had high expectations that lives would change and that people would become who they were called and purposed to be.

In the beginning, I felt alone because this was a new area of ministry for me. My previous life, with no responsibilities as a leader, was behind me, and I was looking at this new role as a leader.

Being an introvert made it even more challenging for me. I prefer being behind the scenes, cheering people on and praying for others. Initially, I wasn't aware of my introversion. I loved people, but I preferred being behind the scenes and at home enjoying myself. I prefer small groups over larger ones. I prefer being at home and focusing on my inner thoughts. I discovered that my introversion was often mistaken for unfriendliness. Being around many people drains an introvert, which is why I need the balance of being alone to rest and get refreshed. I am a leader nonetheless. This is the way that God has wired me, and how I show up as an introverted leader would take some prayer and guidance from the Lord. This is a process.

As my journey continues and I continue to grow in my faith, I have experienced some great blessings and some painful moments because people have imperfections. Because hurting people hurt people, the cycle continues. All of us will offend someone at one time or another. Let's give each other some grace.

The Journey of Intimacy with Jesus

It was in my intimate personal relationship with Jesus and hearing his voice that I became aware of some of my imperfections and issues. I was also made aware of some family cycles that had to be broken.

I want to share a little about one of them.

As a child, I had rage. I would yell and scream and give you a piece of my mind. This continued into my adulthood.

There were times when I was having my moments of rage and being out of control, and I felt a sense of freedom. The truth is that there were times when I really enjoyed it. The older I got, the more it made me feel great to give people a piece of my mind. It gave me a sense of power and control. I called it taking up for myself.

Rage doesn't care if you are male or female; it thinks it can conquer anyone or anything. Rage has a mind of its own, and it tells you how to act and react in certain situations. Rage is ugly! Rage doesn't want to see you succeed in life. Rage is a spirit, and it consumes you in the moment. It leaves you with feelings of regret and remorse because you feel as though that isn't you. Rage has many triggers that, for me, happened suddenly before I was aware of what I was saying or how I reacted in the moment. The triggers are different for each of us.

If I hadn't known Jesus in the way that I did, I don't believe that I would have been set free from that spirit. I had to first acknowledge and not be ashamed that I operated out of a spirit of rage on occasion. I understood that I had to align with God's word in order to be set free, or I would not become who God had destined me to become. I trusted the One who knows me from the inside out. This process wasn't an easy one for me. This wasn't an overnight deliverance; it was an ongoing process of my true surrender and submission to the power of God. Many tears were shed from my eyes. Gradually, I could feel healing in the tears as I continued to surrender to the Lord and commit my ways to Him.

How could God use me to set others free when I needed freedom for myself? This is what drove me. Subconsciously, I knew that this wasn't just for me; it was for my children and generations to come. Was it worth the struggle? Was it worth the pain? Was it worth the fight? My answer is yes. It was worth it. I am seeing the harvest.

God allowed me to be tested in this area of my life. He wasn't trying to kill me; He was trying to mature me and deliver me so that I could become who I am purposed to be and so that I can share my story.

I am grateful to God for the multiple times He allowed me to be tested in the midst of people. He allowed me to be put to the test in the area where I needed deliverance, where I was at the forefront, not in a private setting. Because He knows my strengths and weaknesses, He allowed me to be tested openly. During those tests, I remember thinking, "Oh Lord, not again!" However, they taught me how to lean on Him and trust Him in the moment and not my emotions.

The leader is often thought of as a perfect person who has it all together. On the contrary, the leader experiences life in the same way as others do and often on a higher level of challenges. Leaders have emotions; they experience hurt, betrayal, and alienation. They are flesh and blood, men and women of God assigned to the body of Christ. But the objective of the devil is to kill, steal, and destroy them.

Looking back over my journey, I can understand God's love and protection in ways that I would never have known if I had not surrendered to the process along the journey. It took patience and intentionality on my part. I had to take ownership of my actions. It wasn't enough to pray to God; I needed to partner with God. Rage isn't my portion; peace is!

As I continued to humble myself and to say yes to His will, I began to find myself and the true identity of who I am. I was covered over with anger, rage, and self-doubt for years. Now, my metamorphosis was and still is a process of growth and maturing in my walk with God. It didn't happen overnight—it took years! Some things were harder to be set free from than others. I would fail when tested, but I never gave up. I stayed the course. I was being led by God.

The Awakening

Another level of faith, another level of knowing God's voice. It was an awakening that took me on a new journey of self-discovery! I have shed many tears, and I have felt alone so many times, but I knew that I was being led by the Holy Spirit. Change was needed because He had a plan and purpose for my life. There are many people that I am connected to who need my voice.

Because I didn't have a special mentor in my life, I see the need to reach down and lift someone else up to where they need to be. I have been in settings where you would think that because the anointing of God was in the room, everyone was loving and kind. However, this is the very place where I have been hurt the most. This is the setting where I have been tested the most. I have had to learn how to discern people's motives and not let them affect me so much that they tempt me to quit. The devil's goal was to keep me silent. He has always been after my voice and my influence. Have I always known this? No.

However, I shifted my mindset from victim to victor. This was the opportunity for me to use my voice to help others and see myself how God sees me. The image I had of myself was not the true identity that God has for me. I am being made into His image!!!

I remember going to a women's conference in Atlanta, Georgia. I was in a very long line to get into the event, and some women were pushing and shoving me to get in.

When I got to the front of the line, the lady on duty at the gate grabbed me and pulled me in through the gate. When she grabbed my arm, I still remember not feeling that anger and wanting to come out of God's character. I was calm.

I felt the Lord saying, "Look how far you've come." It showed me that my being intentional and allowing God to change me was not in vain.

And so the journey continues.

When you are hurting inwardly and don't know who to trust, it's challenging. It's a lonely place to be. You do not want to come across as complaining; you just need a trustworthy friend to talk to in a real way.

I can remember hearing people say, "Just pray about it. God will fix it." Well, that is true, but it's not the whole truth. If you do not deal with what's going on within you and you tuck it away and suppress your feelings like they don't matter, then eventually, it turns into harm to your soul and body and results in damage to your mental state of mind as well as your physical body. The pain has to go somewhere. If it's not dealt with in a healthy manner, your spiritual life is also hindered.

The Mask: A Reflection of God's Grace and Power

Looking back over my life and seeing how far God has brought me, I am filled with gratitude. I stand as a living testimony of His grace and the transformative power of trusting Him completely.

Through every season of my life, I have been learning how to place my trust in God. There were seasons on this journey that were incredibly difficult, times when life felt overwhelming, and the path ahead seemed uncertain. During the ups and downs, cloudy days, and struggles, one truth remained constant: I knew that God was with me and working within me.

The journey has been one of discovering and learning who God has created me to be. Painful and disappointing life lessons have shaped me into the woman I am today. Through those hardships, I found joy and purpose.

But there was a time when I wore a mask—a mask that suppressed the fullness of who I am in God. It kept me from moving forward in my walk with the Lord. I suppressed my thoughts and hid the gifts He had given me, and in doing so, I grew bitter—not at God, but at the struggle itself. I was frustrated, angry, and stuck in a place where I couldn't see how to move forward. On the outside, everything may have seemed fine, but on the inside, I was battling thoughts of inadequacy and doubt.

The enemy worked hard to rob me of my voice, silence me, and keep me from walking in my purpose. But one day, I realized something powerful: God gave me my voice, and it does not belong to the enemy. The devil may hinder me, but he cannot stop me because God holds all power.

I've come to understand that everything I went through was allowed by God. Through it all, He was teaching me to listen to His voice and to obey it. Today, I am stronger, bolder, and free to walk in the fullness of who God has called me to be.

To anyone who feels stuck, silenced, or uncertain, I want to encourage you to trust the process. Even in the darkest moments, God is shaping you, refining you, and preparing you for greater things. Let go of the mask and step into his purpose for your life. God's power is greater than any struggle. Trust Him.

It is amazing how we sometimes are out of touch with our feelings and emotions. I believe that I learned how to wear my mask from not wanting to be hurt and for my own protection. The guard went up unknowingly. I didn't realize that I was giving out to others so much that I was neglecting my own mental and spiritual health. I am a servant of the Lord. It was from a place of being a servant and a coach; it was from a place of continually pouring out of my spirit that I missed some opportunities to stop, and I did not pay attention to myself as I should have. I made myself available to God and to others, but I neglected myself in the process. After all, I was called to minister to people, called to minister to people at the point of their need.

When you give from a place of love and seeing the needs of others, you can neglect yourself along the way, and you have to pay a price for it. If the process of giving and serving is not balanced, the scales can tip you over the edge. After some time of neglecting myself, it became evident that it should be dealt with in my daily life. I didn't know this at the beginning of my ministry.

I am thankful that I was and still am able to be that person. I am called to do those things, and I get joy from being able to serve. However, when it was at the expense of my own well-being, it didn't serve me very well,

I can remember times when I felt like I needed a personal break from it all, but I kept moving forward. I learned how to move forward on autopilot. I was on time for services and events and served in different areas of ministry.

Reflecting on my journey, I recognize that I was on autopilot many times. I put false expectations on myself. I didn't have a clear vision of what I was doing to myself and didn't know the toll that it was taking on me. But thank God for His grace.

It is not God's plan for any of us to have false expectations of ourselves and fall into a place where we aren't whole. He is all about us being whole.

As the journey continued and I continued putting myself last, I started to notice changes. My behavior changed slightly at first. I no longer felt joy in what I was doing. The expectations that I once had were now minimal. I had them from time to time, but the joy of the lord was seeping out. The mask became my protector; it protected me from other people. The mask helped me disguise my true feelings, even from myself. The mask hides your imperfections and true identity. It protects you from outside forces. It isolates you and separates you from people.

Yet, my mask was the very thing that saved my life in a very unique way. God protected me from people and incubated me to himself. He covered me under the mask as I was pursuing Him. It became my hiding place spiritually; it was a spiritual incubator that he had me in. I was in a realm with Him that I needed to be. I was inside the incubator looking out. I was alone with God, seemingly lying. I was in two worlds at the same time. Sometimes, the mask is a blessing from God because it is a shield. It is a place of healing from years of challenging moments.

The journey of restoration has begun for me. I trust God's limitless power.

FROM BROKENNESS TO BRILLIANCE

FROM BROKENNESS TO BRILLIANCE

ABOUT THE AUTHOR

MARCY JESSUP

Marcy is a wife, a mother, a grandmother, a great-grandmother, a sister, and a friend.

She is co-founder/co-pastor of Greater Love Fellowship Ministries, where she teaches, preaches, and hosts women's gatherings.

Marcy is called to Pastors' wives.

She studied at Beacon University in Columbia and at the Christian Life School of Ministry. She is an internationally accredited Christian counselor and mental health specialist through Dr.Lashonda Wofford's All Bets On Me Academy.

As the founder of Finding Freedom Consulting Services, LLC, she is passionate about leading others to freedom and helping them to become who they were created to be.

A member of Women in Ministry Support, Marcy prioritizes her family as her first ministry. She loves family time and gains strength from her family. She also loves to have fun, laugh, and sing.

Marcy has spent time encouraging and mentoring others throughout her ministry and understands the importance of meeting people at the point of their need.

CHAPTER 2

IN THE DEPTHS OF DESPAIR:
Coping in the Seasons of Darkness

By Pastor Yolanda Pinkney-Coleman

*"Even though I walk through the darkest valley,
I will fear no evil, for you are with me;
your rod and your staff, they comfort me." (Psalm 23:4, NIV)*

Darkness is an inevitable part of the human experience. Whether we are faced with grief, loss, fear, or anger, we all walk through seasons where despair seems overwhelming. The weight of pain can be suffocating, leaving us feeling isolated and without direction. However, even in the bleakest moments, God's light is never extinguished. It is through faith, perseverance, and the choice to embrace hope that we find healing and restoration.

This chapter explores the emotional toll of suffering, the dangers of unhealthy coping mechanisms, and the importance of anchoring ourselves in God's promises. By understanding our pain and leaning into His presence, we can navigate the depths of despair and emerge stronger.

Life has a way of bringing us to our knees, forcing us to confront the depths of pain we never imagined we could endure. Trauma can emerge from the loss of a loved one, betrayal, abuse, addiction, or sudden life changes that shake us to our core. In these moments, it may feel as though the darkness will never lift, suffocating every ounce of hope we once held onto. I have been in this place, where shadows loom large and despair whispers that there is no way out. But even in these times, God's light is never far away.

Understanding Trauma and Its Grip

Trauma affects us in ways beyond what we can see. It creeps into our minds, shifts our behaviors, and alters the way we perceive ourselves and the world around us. Some people turn to destructive coping mechanisms, seeking relief in substances, isolation, or even self-harm. The enemy uses these moments to tell us we are alone, that no one understands, and that we will never heal. But the truth is that healing is possible, and God's love is greater than any wound we carry.

I had spent years helping others through their pain, guiding, coaching, and ministering to those who had suffered addiction, brokenness, and despair. But now, I was the one drowning, gasping for air in an ocean of sorrow. The loneliness was suffocating. The one person who had always been my rock, my foundation, was gone. I was left staring at the empty chair where she once sat, feeling the cruel reality of absence settle deep into my bones.

A Love That Shaped Me

My mother was my first friend, my greatest protector, and my most consistent supporter. As an only child, she was my world, and I was hers. The bond we shared needed no words; it was built on love, sacrifice, and an unbreakable connection. She was my safe place, my source of wisdom, and the foundation of my faith.

When I lost her, it felt like my world had collapsed. The pain was more than grief—it was a hollowness that stretched deep into my soul. There were days I could barely breathe, nights I couldn't sleep, and moments where the silence of my new reality was deafening. Losing a mother is never easy, but losing her as an only child left me feeling completely alone.

It was in those dark moments that I truly understood what despair felt like. It is the kind of sorrow that steals your joy, drains your strength, and leaves you questioning everything you once believed. I had counseled many through grief and prayed for others in their seasons of loss, but now I was the one needing the prayers.

> "The Lord is close to the brokenhearted
> and saves those who are crushed in spirit." — Psalm 34:18 (NIV)

I clung to scriptures like this, hoping they would ease the pain, but at times, even my faith felt fragile. I wondered, *God, where are You in this? Why does this hurt so much?*

The Emotional Toll of Pain

Grief is not just sadness; it's a storm of emotions that come in unpredictable waves.

Fear

Fear gripped me in ways I had never experienced before. Losing my mother meant losing my foundation, my guide, my unwavering support. I feared the loneliness that came with being an only child without parents. Who would I call when I needed wisdom? Who would remind me of my worth when the world tried to tear me down?

Fear whispered lies in my ear, telling me I wouldn't be able to handle life without her, that I would crumble under the weight of my grief. It told me I was alone and that no one could possibly understand my pain.

But in those moments of overwhelming fear, I clung to Isaiah 41:10, which says: *"Fear not, for I am with you; be not dismayed, for I am your God; I will strengthen you, I will help you, I will uphold you with my righteous right hand."*

God reminded me that though my earthly mother was gone, He had never left me. He was still my refuge, my safe place. But it took time before I could fully embrace that truth.

Loss

The weight of loss is suffocating. It's not just the loss of a person, but the loss of identity, the loss of security, the loss of the future you imagined with them. My mother was more than just my mom—she was my best friend, my biggest cheerleader. Losing her meant losing a part of myself.

There were days I didn't want to get out of bed. I didn't want to answer calls or engage in life. The world kept moving, but mine had stopped. It felt unfair—why did the world get to go on while I was stuck in this pit of sorrow?

I found comfort in Psalm 34:18: *"The Lord is near to the brokenhearted and saves the crushed in spirit."*

Even in my loss, God was there. Even when I couldn't feel Him, He was holding me together when I wanted to fall apart.

My mother was not just a person; she was my history, my storyteller, and my safe place. I grieved the holidays we would never spend together, the advice I would never hear again, and the simple moments we once shared—her laughter, hugs, cooking, and the way she called my name.

I found myself wanting to pick up the phone to call her, only to be hit with the cruel reality that she was no longer here. The loss was both physical and emotional, and it felt like losing a piece of myself.

Fear: The Paralyzing Force

Fear thrives in uncertainty. It tells us we are alone, vulnerable, and without hope. When fear consumes us, it can cloud our judgment and prevent us from trusting God's plan.

> *"For God has not given us a spirit of fear, but of power and of love and of a sound mind." (2 Timothy 1:7, NKJV)*

When the disciples found themselves in a storm, they cried out in fear, "Lord, save us! We're going to drown!" (Matthew 8:25). Yet, Jesus responded, "You of little faith, why are you so afraid?" (Matthew 8:26). His words remind us that even in the chaos, He is in control.

Anger: A Fire That Consumes

Anger is often a reaction to injustice, betrayal, or deep hurt. While anger itself is not sinful, allowing it to fester leads to destruction.

> *"In your anger do not sin: Do not let the sun go down while you are still angry" (Ephesians 4:26, NIV)*

Moses, a leader chosen by God, struggled with anger. His temper led to striking the rock instead of speaking to it as God commanded (Numbers 20:10-12). This disobedience cost him entry into the Promised Land. His story warns us of the consequences of unchecked anger and the importance of surrendering our emotions to God.

Anger was perhaps the most unexpected emotion. I was angry at the world for moving on. I was angry at friends who didn't check in. I was angry at the doctors for not saving her. And, if I'm being honest, I was angry at God.

"Why did You take her?" "Why didn't You heal her?" "Why did You leave me alone?"

These questions swirled in my mind, and for a time, I let my anger push me away from God. But in my brokenness, He met me. He didn't condemn me for my anger. Instead, He gently reminded me that He understood. Even Jesus wept when Lazarus died (John 11:35). Even Jesus cried out, *"My God, My God, why have You forsaken Me?"* (Matthew 27:46).

God wasn't offended by my pain. He invited me to bring it to Him, to lay it at His feet.

Grief

Grief is a natural response to loss, whether it be the passing of a loved one, the end of a relationship, or the collapse of a dream. It can feel like an unrelenting storm, with waves of sorrow crashing unexpectedly. Many biblical figures experienced profound grief, yet God remained their refuge.

> *"Blessed are those who mourn, for they will be comforted"*
> *(Matthew 5:4, NIV)*

David, a man after God's own heart, poured out his sorrow through psalms. In Psalm 42:11, he cries, "Why, my soul, are you downcast? Why so disturbed within me? Put your hope in God, for I will yet praise him, my Savior and my God." His example teaches us that lamenting before God is not a sign of weakness but an act of faith.

Grief does not introduce itself gently. It does not knock on the door and ask permission to enter. It crashes in like an unrelenting storm, uprooting everything you once knew to be stable. The pain of loss was immediate, but its depth only grew as the days turned into weeks and the weeks into months.

Grief is not a straight path; it's a winding road with highs and lows, good days and unbearable ones. Some days, I could smile at her memory, and other days, I could barely get out of bed.

I had to remind myself that grief is not a sign of weakness—it's a reflection of love. The deeper the love, the deeper the grief.

> *"Blessed are those who mourn, for they will be comforted."*
> *— Matthew 5:4 (NIV)*

Grief is not linear. It is unpredictable, messy, and deeply personal. Some days, I felt numb. Other days, a song, a scent, or an old voicemail would send me spiraling. There is no timeline for healing, no magic formula to make it hurt less.

But I found solace in Lamentations 3:22-23: *"The steadfast love of the Lord never ceases; His mercies never come to an end; they are new every morning; great is Your faithfulness."*

Even in grief, God's mercies were new each day. Even in sorrow, His love remained.

The Struggle to Cope

The pain of grief can lead us to seek relief in unhealthy ways. Some may withdraw from loved ones, choosing isolation over connection. Others may turn to temporary escapes—numbing the pain through substances, work, or distractions that ultimately leave the heart even more empty. The temptation to revert to old habits or destructive coping mechanisms can be strong, especially when grief feels unbearable.

As someone who has walked the road of recovery, I know how easy it is to fall into despair. The enemy whispers lies, tempting us to believe that the pain will never subside and that hope is lost. But I have also experienced the power of God's grace—how He gently pulls us back when we surrender our pain to Him. Healing is not found in avoidance but in allowing ourselves to feel, to process, and ultimately, to trust that God's plan is greater than our understanding.

When faced with despair, many turn to destructive habits as a means of escape. These coping mechanisms offer temporary relief but ultimately deepen our wounds.

Isolation

Suffering often tempts us to withdraw from others. We convince ourselves that no one understands our pain. Yet, isolation fuels despair.

> *"Two are better than one, because they have a good return for their labor: If either of them falls down, one can help the other up"* (Ecclesiastes 4:9-10, NIV)

God created us for community. Even Jesus, in His darkest hour, sought the presence of His disciples in Gethsemane (Matthew 26:36-38).

Substance Abuse

Many seek solace in drugs or alcohol, numbing their pain instead of addressing it. However, reliance on substances only deepens the wounds.

> *"Do not get drunk on wine, which leads to debauchery. Instead, be filled with the Spirit." (Ephesians 5:18, NIV)*

God calls us to be filled with His presence rather than seeking artificial comfort.

Bitterness and Resentment

Holding onto bitterness prevents healing. It traps us in a cycle of anger and pain.

> *"Get rid of all bitterness, rage and anger... Be kind and compassionate to one another, forgiving each other, just as in Christ God forgave you" (Ephesians 4:31-32, NIV)*

Choosing forgiveness, though difficult, frees us from the chains of resentment.

Pride and pain are a dangerous combination. I had spent so many years being the strong one, the one others leaned on. Now, in my own time of need, I found it difficult to reach out. I withdrew from friends, avoided phone calls, and isolated myself in my grief. The lie that whispered in my ear was, *No one understands. No one truly cares.*

But isolation only deepens despair. It traps you in a cycle of loneliness, feeding the very pain you are trying to escape.

When grief feels unbearable, it's tempting to escape it—anything to numb the pain. For me, the temptation to relapse after 29 years of sobriety was real. The thought whispered in my mind: *"One drink won't hurt." "You just need something to take the edge off." "You deserve relief."*

The enemy knows our weaknesses, and in our weakest moments, he plants seeds of destruction. But I knew deep down that numbing the pain wouldn't heal me. It would only push me further from the healing I desperately needed.

Proverbs 3:5-6 reminded me: *"Trust in the Lord with all your heart, and do not lean on your own understanding. In all your ways acknowledge Him, and He will make straight your paths."*

Turning to substances wouldn't bring my mother back. It wouldn't ease the grief. It would only add more chains to the weight I was already carrying.

Another dangerous coping mechanism was isolation. I withdrew from people who cared about me, thinking that no one could possibly understand my pain. But that only deepened my despair.

Ecclesiastes 4:9-10 says: *"Two are better than one... If either of them falls down, one can help the other up. But pity anyone who falls and has no one to help them up."*

I had to choose to reach out, to let people in, even when it felt impossible.

Even in the darkness, there were glimpses of light. Little reminders that God was still with me, still holding me, still guiding me through.

I found hope in the memories of my mother's love, in the strength she passed down to me, and in the lessons she taught me.

I found hope in scripture, in prayer, in worship. I found hope in the people who supported me, the kindness of my friends, and also the gentle ways God reminded me that I was not alone.

One of the most powerful moments of hope came when I realized that my mother's legacy lived on in me. She had poured so much into me—her faith, her wisdom, her resilience. And even though she was gone, those things remained.

"Weeping may endure for a night, but joy comes in the morning."
— Psalm 30:5 (KJV)

Grief doesn't mean the end of joy. Healing doesn't mean forgetting. And pain doesn't mean God has abandoned us.

One of the most powerful revelations in my journey was understanding that my pain had a purpose. God never allows us to go through trials without using them for His kingdom. My own experiences with trauma, addiction, and loss became a testimony—proof that God can redeem even the darkest seasons of our lives.

As I began to walk in my purpose, I realized that everything I had endured was not just for me—it was for those I would one day minister to. Every battle, every scar, and every victory became a tool to help others find their own healing.

Your pain is not wasted. God will use your story to bring hope to someone else. What the enemy meant for evil, God will turn for good.

The journey toward hope begins with surrender. We often hold onto our trauma because we don't know how to release it. We carry burdens that were never meant to be ours alone. In Matthew 11:28, Jesus says, *"Come to me, all who are weary and burdened, and I will give you rest."* Surrendering does not mean forgetting; it means placing our pain in the hands of the One who can heal us completely. Through prayer, worship, and seeking God's presence, we begin to see the cracks of dawn in our darkest night.

One of the greatest lies trauma tells us is that we must go through it alone. The enemy thrives in isolation, but healing happens in community. Surrounding ourselves with those who can pray for us, encourage us, and hold us accountable is a vital step in our journey. Faith-based support groups, church families, mentors, and even professional counseling can provide the guidance and encouragement we need to push forward.

Healing does not mean we will never feel pain again, but it does mean we are no longer bound by it. The chains of trauma do not define us. "So if the Son sets you free, you will be free indeed" (John 8:36). We are not our past mistakes, our deepest wounds, or our darkest days. Through Christ, we are renewed, restored, and redeemed. There is power in reclaiming our identity in God and walking boldly into His promises.

There are moments in life when time seems to stand still, when the very air around you changes, signaling that nothing will ever be the same again. The day my mother took her last breath was one of those moments.

Loss has a way of creeping in like a slow-moving storm, dark and ominous. At first, it was disbelief. I kept expecting to hear her voice on the other end of the phone or to see her number pop up with a text reminding me to eat or take a break from my busy day. But the silence was deafening. The reality hit in waves—she was gone. And nothing I did could change that.

I found myself trapped in the depths of despair, drowning in a sea of emotions I didn't know how to navigate. Fear, loss, anger, and grief became my constant companions. I was no stranger to hardship, but this was different. This loss was intimate and profound, and it left me feeling abandoned.

Hope doesn't always come as a grand revelation. Sometimes, it's in the small things—a sunrise, a kind word, a memory that brings a smile instead of tears.

One of the most powerful truths I clung to was Romans 8:28:

"And we know that in all things God works for the good of those who love Him, who have been called according to His purpose."

Even in my pain, God was working. Even in my grief, He had a plan.

Slowly, I began to see glimpses of light in the darkness. I found comfort in worship, prayer, and journaling my emotions. I started to thank God—not for the loss, but for the years I had with my mother, for the love she gave me, for the legacy she left behind.

God never promised a life without sorrow, but He promised to be with us in it. Psalm 30:5 says:

"Weeping may endure for a night, but joy comes in the morning."

Morning doesn't always come quickly, but it does come. Healing is a process, but God is faithful.

Losing my mother changed me. Grief is now a part of my story, but it does not define me. I am still standing, not because I am strong, but because God's strength carried me.

I share my story not because I have all the answers but because I want others to know they are not alone. If you are grieving, if you feel like you are drowning in despair, know this:

God sees you. God loves you. And He will carry you through.

Hold onto His promises. Trust that joy will come again. And remember, even in the depths of despair, God is still there.

FROM BROKENNESS TO BRILLIANCE

ABOUT THE AUTHOR

PASTOR YOLANDA PINKNEY-COLEMAN

Meet Pastor Yolanda "Monique" Pinkney-Coleman, a native New Yorker born and raised in South Jamaica, Queens. A devoted servant of the Lord for over twenty-eight years, Pastor Yolanda accepted her public call to ministry in 1999 during her pregnancy with her last child. She received her Evangelist/Missionary License under the leadership of Elder Solomon Bryant of Second St. Paul's Church of Christ, Disciple of Christ, in Brooklyn, NY. She has served in several ministry capacities, including outreach, prison ministry, the Missionary Board, and as an Armorbearer. Pastor Yolanda eventually relocated to Richmond, VA, in 2001. Through divine revelation and a transformative encounter during a women's conference, she told God "Yes" and submitted humbly to God's will for her life and ministry. She has since been licensed as a minister, ordained as an Elder, and installed as a Pastor in 2021.

Pastor Yolanda "Monique" Pinkney-Coleman is a Senior Pastor of Restoration Assemblies Outreach Ministries of North Carolina and New York City. She serves alongside her husband, Pastor Jerome E. Coleman. They identify themselves as "Team Coleman." Pastor Yolanda's ministry focuses on Healing, Deliverance, and Outreach. She firmly believes that the Bible is the inspired Word of God, holding the answers to all of life's challenges. Her love for God and His people drives her unwavering dedication to reaching out to the poor, oppressed, brokenhearted, and orphaned.

With over twenty-five years of experience in the Human Service field, specializing in substance abuse, mental health, and recovery, Pastor Yolanda is a Board-Certified Mental Health Coach, Substance Abuse Recovery Coach, Life Purpose Coach, Mentor, and Entrepreneur. Her mission is to guide at-risk youth, teens, and young adults through their struggles with addiction, mental health disorders, adverse childhood experiences, trauma, domestic violence, and reintegration into society after incarceration. She is a motivational speaker, podcaster, and advocate.

Pastor Yolanda's motto, "Be Stronger Than Your Excuses," reflects her belief in the power of determination and perseverance. Pastor Yolanda pursued her education in Human Services, Substance Abuse, Psychology, Christian Counseling, biblical studies, and K-6 teaching. She has also undergone chaplaincy training.

Pastor Yolanda shares a blended family of eight adult children, fourteen grandchildren, and one great-granddaughter with her husband, Pastor Jerome Coleman. They are dedicated speakers and hosts of the online podcast "L.I.F.E. (Living in Freedom Everyday)." Her literary contributions include books such as "From Broken to Reborn," "Road to Recovery: Predestined for a Purpose," "Road to Recovery Prayer Journal," and contributions to "Queens Chronicles: A Letter to My Sister Queens, Part I."

Pastor Yolanda Pinkney-Coleman's life is a testament to her unwavering faith, compassion, and commitment to serving others. She aspires to bring healing, deliverance, and freedom to the lives she touches, guided by the belief that no obstacle is insurmountable with God by your side.

CHAPTER 3

FROM BROKENNESS TO BRILLIANCE:

Finding Purpose and Passion Beyond Your Pain

By Sandra Wolf

"Weeping may endure for the night, but joy comes in the morning." - Psalm 30:5

This truth became my anchor through the storm of grief and loss, reminding me that even in my darkest moments, God had a plan for my restoration.

In 2018, my world began to shake when I was diagnosed with breast cancer. I faced the fear, the uncertainty, and the grueling treatments that left me physically and emotionally drained. But I fought. I clung to faith and the belief that I had a purpose beyond my pain.

Just as I thought I had overcome one battle, another storm came crashing into my life. August 2019 was supposed to be another ordinary month, another moment in time where love and hope carried me forward. That morning, I received a text from my husband, Antonio: "Good morning, Queen. Can't wait to see you tomorrow." Those words, filled with love and anticipation, would be the last message I ever received from him.

At 6:30 PM, my world shattered when I got a frantic call telling me I needed to come to South Carolina immediately—something had happened to Antonio. My heart pounded as I raced against time, desperately praying that it was all a misunderstanding.

As I was driving to South Carolina, I kept repeating, "God, take the wheel." And He did. That night, what should have been a two-hour drive felt like a blur. Antonio's hometown didn't have a hospital, so they had to take him to the next town. The roads were dark, my mind was clouded, and I barely remembered what I packed—I just threw clothes into a bag and left.

When I arrived at the hospital, I saw people standing outside like it was a tailgate party. My gut told me the truth before anyone else could: My sweet husband was gone. Have you ever watched a Lifetime movie where the woman hears tragic news and collapses onto the floor as if her body can't hold her up? I always thought those scenes were exaggerated—until I lived it myself.

I stepped out of the SUV and immediately fell to the ground. Antonio's brother and sister rushed to pick me up, helping me inside. I thought a doctor was approaching me, but it was the coroner instead. That was the moment I truly lost it. The weight of reality hit me like a tidal wave, and I crumbled under its force. The coroner took the family into a room and told them, "I am going to talk to the wife." He gave me some time to compose myself and then asked if I had any questions. I didn't know what to ask—my mind was all over the place. He advised that there was not going to be an autopsy because the cause of death was clear: Antonio had been stung 30 to 35 times by yellow jackets. With that many stings and without anyone having access to an EpiPen, the venom quickly overwhelmed his system. An EpiPen is used to treat severe allergic reactions, including anaphylaxis, which can be life-threatening. However, Antonio was not allergic to bees, and I don't keep an EpiPen in my home either—like many people who don't have known allergies.

Most individuals who carry an EpiPen do so because they or someone close to them has a known allergy to things like food, insect stings, or medications. Even if one had been available and used, there's no guarantee it would have saved his life, given the extreme number of stings he suffered. In cases of mass envenomation like this, the sheer volume of venom can cause toxic reactions even in individuals without allergies, leading to cardiac arrest, organ failure, or other fatal complications.

This tragic event serves as a reminder of how dangerous multiple stings can be—not just for those with allergies but for anyone exposed to a significant amount of venom.

My reality was cruel. He was gone. Just like that, the man who had stood by my side for 13 years and who had loved me unconditionally had been taken from me without warning.

Antonio had been in his mother's yard on a beautiful day, enjoying time with friends and family near a large tree. Suddenly, a swarm of yellow jackets emerged from the ground and attacked him while he was sweeping with a broom. He ran around the house trying to fend them off before seeking refuge inside, reassuring his mother that he was alright.

Moments later, he stood up, walked into the living room, and collapsed. Despite the ambulance being called promptly, he tragically passed away before reaching the hospital. His sudden loss deeply shocked everyone; we mourned the loss of a son, brother, and friend, and I lost my beloved husband. The mystery of the nest, which was never found despite the incident, added to the profound sense of disbelief and sadness we all felt.

In the days that followed, I had no time to think about myself—I had a funeral to plan. Despite my grief, I focused on honoring Antonio. I drove back and forth to get his burial suit. He had always said he didn't want a grave marker; he didn't live his life in a box, and he didn't want to be buried in one either—he wanted to be cremated. On the day of the funeral, my sisters and mother stayed in a hotel that one of Antonio's family members paid for, and I was so grateful. My little sister did my makeup—soft and natural. I wore a dark red dress. That morning, I prayed, "Lord, let me walk in grace." And I did. He carried me.

After the funeral, I said goodbye to Antonio's family, and my family and I returned to Georgia. I walked into an empty house—without my husband. I would never hear his laughter again, never have him beside me at night, and never share the simple, everyday moments that we often take for granted. He had always been the cook in our home—I still don't enjoy cooking to this day. He cooked, and I took out the trash. I will say this: Keep people out of your marriage and relationships, and do what makes your house happy and what works for you both! And now, the silence in our home was deafening.

Weeks or maybe months later, I drove back to South Carolina to pick up Antonio's ashes and give some to his family members. The rest I took back home with me in a vase. Later, I went to a beautiful river in Roswell, Georgia, and scattered some of his ashes there. I prayed. I cried. I laughed. I kept a small amount in a bag, and whenever I traveled, I took a little with me to spread in the ocean. Antonio now rests in Spain, Germany, the Dominican Republic, and other places. He didn't live his life in a box, and in death, I made sure he never would.

As the days went on, I kept asking myself: *How do I go on?* But you find a way. Grief is not a linear journey. It is a storm that rages in waves, knocking you down just when you think you've found your footing. I cycled through the five stages of grief all at once—denial, anger, bargaining, depression, and finally, a reluctant acceptance. I questioned everything. *How could God allow this to happen? How could I go on without him?*

There is a story often told about a person walking along the beach with God. Scenes from their life played out before them, and as they looked down, they noticed two sets of footprints in the sand—one belonging to them and one to God. But in the lowest moments of their life, only one set of footprints remained. They asked God, "Why did you leave me when I needed you the most?" And God answered, "My child, I never left you. Those were the moments I carried you."

That story became my reality. In the moments when I felt like I couldn't take another step, God carried me through the kindness of friends, the strength I didn't know I possessed, and the whisper of hope that told me I was not alone.

Slowly, I began to find purpose beyond my pain. My journey—through cancer and grief—was not meant to be hidden. It was meant to be shared, to be a beacon of hope for others who felt lost in the darkness. I began speaking to widows, to women facing loss and fear, reminding them that life does not end with tragedy. We are allowed to mourn and break, but we are also allowed to rise, rebuild, and rediscover our passion.

One of the affirmations that carried me through was: "I am not what happened to me; I am what I choose to become." I repeated this daily, reminding myself that though my story included pain, it did not have to end in despair.

Grief is a transformation. It changes you, but it does not have to define you. I found solace in writing, helping others, and speaking life into those who felt like their world had ended because I was once there. But I am here now, standing in the brilliance of a life reborn.

FROM BROKENNESS TO BRILLIANCE

ABOUT THE AUTHOR

SANDRA WOLF
– More Than a Widow, Turning Pain Into Purpose

Sandra Wolf was born in Germany and moved to the United States at the age of seven. Her journey has been shaped by resilience, faith, and an unwavering commitment to uplifting others. From an early age, she experienced profound loss, including the devastating suicide of her father and the passing of her younger sister to leukemia—though she was too young to remember her. Despite these tragedies, Sandra has chosen to turn her pain into purpose, walking by faith and striving to bring light to others.

But Sandra is more than a widow. She is a sister, an aunt, a daughter, a friend, a businesswoman, and a faith-driven woman who continues to push forward despite life's challenges. While she is strong, she also has her sad moments—times when grief weighs heavy. But through it all, she chooses to keep going, to lift others up, and to remind people that they are never alone in their struggles.

Sandra comes from a close-knit family, including her twin sister, a younger sister who is ten years her junior, and a beloved niece and nephew. Her mother, who remains one of the most important figures in her life, still resides in Germany. Though their relationship was not always easy, God has mended their bond, and they now cherish a deep connection. Her mother flies to the United States each year to visit, strengthening their loving relationship despite the miles between them.

A firm believer in spreading positivity, Sandra finds joy in lifting others. Whether complimenting a stranger at Walmart or offering a word of encouragement, she believes in the power of kindness. In a world filled with negativity, she chooses to be a source of light, understanding that even the smallest gestures can give someone hope.

Faith is the foundation of Sandra's life. She acknowledges that the path has not always been easy and has faced moments of questioning and frustration with God. Yet, she trusts in His plan, knowing that everything unfolds as it is meant to. As she continues her journey, she focuses less on the opinions of others and more on aligning herself with God's purpose—living boldly, embracing peace, and inspiring others to do the same.

The most defining moment of Sandra's life came in August 2019 with the sudden loss of her husband, Antonio. This tragedy became the catalyst for her mission to help others navigate grief in an honest, raw, and transformative way. Traditional conversations about loss often felt inadequate, failing to capture the true emotional rollercoaster of losing a spouse. Determined to create a space for widows and those experiencing profound grief, she founded a movement to provide support, healing, and community.

Her first book, *Grief After Losing Your King! There Are Stages to This Shit! Some Facts,* was born out of this passion. In it, she breaks down the nonlinear, messy stages of grief—the heartbreak, anger, guilt, and, eventually, the moments of light that begin to emerge. Sandra's message is clear: Grief does not define us. While the pain never fully disappears, we learn to carry it differently, finding strength in the chaos and rebuilding ourselves one step at a time.

Beyond her book, Sandra has expanded her movement with uplifting products designed to encourage healing and self-reflection. Her brand includes positive affirmation magnets, guided journals to help track personal growth, and empowering apparel such as T-shirts and sweatshirts. As her platform grows, so does her mission to reach more people who need support in their grief journey.

Sandra's story is proof that life can change in an instant, but it is also a testament to the resilience of the human spirit. She is living proof that while loss can shape you, it does not have to break you. Her goal is to remind others that they are not alone—that together, they can navigate the stages of grief and rediscover life in a way that honors their lost loved ones while embracing their own future.

Connect with Sandra:

✉@ Email: Queen.Sandra.Wolf@gmail.com

📷 Instagram: @Royal_Brand_Sandra.333

🌐 Website: https://www.royalty-sw.com/

CHAPTER 4

BEYOND THE VERDICT:
A Journey from Pain to Power

By Dr. Iris Wright

"When a woman finds her strength, she finds her identity."
– Dr. Iris Wright

In the summer of 1999, beneath the vibrant hues of July skies, my life shifted irrevocably. At sixteen, I welcomed a beautiful baby girl into the world. In that moment—radiant with joy yet shadowed by fear—a new chapter began. Motherhood arrived without warning, demanding a strength and resilience I had yet to discover. This is not merely the story of becoming a mother. It is a testament to how, through the trials and triumphs of that journey, I uncovered my true identity. In the crucible of hardship and sacrifice, I transformed, emerging with a fierce, unbreakable power.

Early Motherhood: Sacrifice and Survival

Motherhood at sixteen thrust me into an arena of responsibilities I scarcely understood. The fragile weight of my newborn daughter in my arms ignited a protective love within me that reshaped my very being. Dreams of a conventional teenage life evaporated. When Delaware's labor laws restricted my work hours, I faced an agonizing decision: leaving school to provide for her. The vision of crossing the graduation stage faded—replaced by a far greater purpose: giving my daughter a future filled with opportunity.

My days became a balancing act of exhaustion and determination. Dawn found me rising early for work, and the late hours of the night were devoted to caregiving. Each dollar stretched thin; each meal was planned with precision. Though physically drained, I drew strength from the example of my mother—a single parent who, through grit and sacrifice, raised her children against the odds. I vowed to break the cycle of hardship, determined that my daughter would have more than I ever had.

To cope, I leaned on moments of reflection and small victories. I became resourceful, learning to find opportunities where none seemed to exist. While others saw only a young girl struggling, I saw myself evolving—growing wiser with every challenge. I carried the seeds of transformation within me, though I did not yet understand the depth of my resilience.

Books became my solace. In those moments of isolation, I immersed myself in self-education, clinging to the belief that knowledge would open doors. Each challenge became an opportunity to grow, and each victory was a sign that the life I dreamed of for us was within reach. I understood that success would come not in grand leaps but in small, persistent steps forward.

Separation and the Cost of Love

Time brought unforeseen changes. My relationship with my daughter's father deteriorated under the weight of conflicting priorities. As I searched for stable housing, I faced another agonizing choice—temporarily placing my daughter in her father's care. Though it was done out of love, the separation deeply wounded my soul. Every day apart felt interminable. I clung to the memories of her laughter, the warmth of her tiny hand in mine, and the unbreakable bond we shared.

Despite the pain, I kept my eyes on the future. This period of separation was a necessary step—a way to build a stronger foundation for both of us. I constantly reminded myself that sacrifice is sometimes the price of progress. In the quiet moments of reflection, I reaffirmed my resolve. I would not be defeated.

I stayed connected through letters, phone calls, and brief visits. I cherished every update about her growth and each milestone she reached in my absence. Though my heart ached with longing, I knew our separation was temporary. This knowledge fueled my determination to fight harder and rebuild a home where we could be together again.

The Emergency That Changed Everything

One autumn evening brought both hope and calamity. Reunited with my daughter, I noticed alarming sores on her delicate skin. Urgency seized me. I rushed her to the doctor, who diagnosed her with impetigo, a bacterial skin infection. With a prescription in hand, I set out to ensure her recovery. Yet, life's relentless trials continued. My job, already precarious, demanded my presence. Torn between work and motherhood, I made the difficult decision to leave my daughter in her father's care for the day, vowing to return for her as soon as possible.

That choice set off a devastating chain of events. A mother's worst fear is not just losing her child but losing the ability to protect her. The events that followed would test every ounce of my resolve.

Accusations and Betrayal

Accusations have a way of shattering trust. When false ones arise, the pain deepens tenfold. A phone call delivered the blow: I was accused of neglecting my daughter. Love and responsibility were twisted into a narrative of failure and harm. Shackled by a justice system that saw only suspicion, I faced criminal charges that threatened to sever the most sacred bond of my life.

A public defender believed in my innocence, but the system loomed large and unfeeling. A plea deal was offered—a compromise that would stain my name forever. I refused. My spirit rejected the notion of surrender. I chose to fight, taking my battle to the courtroom.

The Trial: Fighting for the Truth

The courtroom became my battlefield. The judge, a figure of authority and discernment, saw through the distortions. His direct questions pierced the fog of bureaucracy. I answered with unwavering truth, my voice steady and resolute. My words carried the weight of maternal love and the unshakable conviction that I had done everything to protect my daughter.

Justice, though slow, partially prevailed. Most charges were dropped, though one remained—a scar upon my record but not upon my spirit. Probation became a small price for the chance to reclaim my life. As I walked out of the courtroom, a mix of relief and fierce determination filled me. My battle was not over; it had merely evolved.

Redemption and Reunion

In February 2006, the moment I had fought for finally arrived. My daughter was returned to my care. Our reunion was a tidal wave of emotion—tears, laughter, and the overwhelming joy of holding her again. Yet, life soon tested us once more. A health scare emerged, casting shadows over our newfound peace. I remained vigilant, standing as her guardian through countless medical appointments and sleepless nights.

These challenges revealed depths of strength I had never imagined. I was no longer just a mother; I was a warrior for my daughter's safety and happiness. Our bond, strengthened by adversity, became the cornerstone of our journey forward.

We rebuilt our lives one step at a time. The laughter of a child filled our home again. I savored the simple moments—helping with homework, playing in the park, and tucking her in at night. Each day was a testament to our shared resilience.

Pursuit of Justice: Pardon and Vindication

Though reunited, the scars of my legal battle persisted. Determined to clear my name, I sought a pardon. The initial rejection was crushing, but it only steeled my resolve. Years later, a compassionate board member saw the truth of my transformation. With her support, my case gained momentum, culminating in a pardon signed by Governor John C. Carney. The weight of years of injustice was lifted, replaced by the liberating light of vindication.

The process was not just about clearing my record. It was about reclaiming my voice and rewriting the narrative of my life. I became an advocate for others facing similar struggles, sharing my story to inspire hope and change.

Turning Pain into Power

Healing is neither simple nor linear, but it is powerful. Over time, I embraced my journey, viewing my scars as symbols of resilience rather than wounds. I became the Black Diamond—a gem forged under immense pressure, shining with strength and beauty.

Today, I stand as Dr. Iris Wright: a wife, mother, grandmother, entrepreneur, author, and advocate for social justice. I have turned my pain into purpose, inspiring others to find their power in the face of hardship. My message is clear: no matter how dark the journey is, there is always light at the end.

FROM BROKENNESS TO BRILLIANCE

ABOUT THE AUTHOR

DR. IRIS WRIGHT
A Visionary Entrepreneur and Advocate for Change

Dr. Iris Wright stands at the forefront of entrepreneurial innovation and community advocacy, with an impressive portfolio that includes *Caring Hearts Telecare, Caring Hearts Foundation, Caring Hearts Telecoach, Wrights Virtual Services, Wrights Holdings,* and her influential platforms: *Author Iris Wright, Real Talk with Iris,* and *Black Diamond Chronicle Magazine.* Married for 13 years, Dr. Wright is the matriarch of a blended family with six children and three grandchildren. Six years ago, she relocated from Delaware to Newport News, Virginia, seeking new opportunities and fresh beginnings.

Iris's entrepreneurial spirit and passion for service emerged early in her life, setting the foundation for her dynamic career. After a decade in restaurant management and various roles, her true calling in healthcare emerged at 28, sparking a heartfelt mission to care for others.

In 2019, inspired by Steve Harvey's "Jump," Iris made the bold decision to pursue full-time entrepreneurship, launching Wright's Virtual Services. Her entrepreneurial leap continued with the creation of Caring Hearts Senior Living in January 2021, later rebranded as Caring Hearts Telecare in July 2022, earning a nomination for Best Home Care of the Year 2023 and 2024 in Newport News, VA.

Dr. Wright's influence extends beyond her businesses. In July 2022, she was invited to speak on Telehealth in Home Care at a Leading Age seminar, demonstrating her innovative approach to elder care. Her leadership and community impact have garnered multiple accolades in 2023, including *the Community Leader Award from ACHI Magazine,* the Phenomenal Women Award from My Sisters Keeper, the Empowered Diva Award, and recognition as Author All-Star of the Year and Top 20 Author of the Year from Book Profits Club. Additionally, she was honored with the 2023 Community Votes Award, the 2024 Community Votes Award, and two Honorary Doctorates in Healthcare Administration and Business. In 2024, Dr. Wright will receive the prestigious Black Excellence Award, the Presidential Lifetime Achievement Award, the Woman of the Year Award, and the International Impact Award. She was listed in Forbes Top 20 Entrepreneurs to close out 2024.

Her literary contributions, including best-sellers such as *Taking Your Power Back*, *Win in Nursing*, *What Is Fearless Living*, *Girl Don't Count Yourself Out*, and *Joy 365*, reflect her dedication to empowering others. Her upcoming solo works, *Injustice: My Story* and *Evolving the Storm*, delve deep into her personal journey of overcoming adversity. With her visionary projects like *Black Diamond Chronicles*, *Injustice Vol II*, and *Teen Mom to Entrepreneur* set to launch in 2025, Dr. Wright continues to inspire through her writing.

In addition to her entrepreneurial achievements, Dr. Wright is a passionate advocate for affordable Home Care and fair reimbursement rates for seniors, ensuring the elderly receive quality care. Her Injustice Movement, launched in January 2023, exemplifies her commitment to social justice, offering legal support to the wrongly accused and working to reunite families. Dr. Wright is currently assisting in the fight for clemency for a man who has served 27 years of an 80-year sentence for a non-violent crime.

Dr. Iris Wright's unwavering dedication to community, justice, and innovation has made her a beacon of hope and change. Through her ventures, writing, and advocacy, she continues to inspire others to leap into their purpose and transform lives.

Connect with Dr. Iris Wright:

- Website: [iris-wright.com] (https://www.iris-wright.com/)
- Facebook: [Author Iris Wright] (https://www.facebook.com/authoririswright)
- Instagram: [@author_iris_wright] (https://www.instagram.com/author_iris_wright/)

CHAPTER 5

TURNING PAIN INTO PURPOSE:
Peace over panic, Faith over Fear, Wisdom Over Worry!

By Dawanna Alexander

"God is in the midst of her; she shall not be moved: God shall help her, and that right early" (Psalm 46:5)

Understanding how challenges shape your mission.

As I reflect on my life, I am reminded that even during the periods when I did not have a relationship with God, He has always remained steadfast and present in my life. I am deeply grateful for God's unwavering presence, as I can confidently attest that without Him, I would not have been able to overcome the numerous challenges that I have faced along the way.

Throughout my life, I have encountered a multitude of obstacles that would have led many individuals to succumb to despair. However,

God's divine strength empowered me to persevere and triumph over adversity. As I continue to anchor my faith in the Word of God, I am filled with an overwhelming sense of purpose, which motivates me to assist others in recognizing that regardless of the circumstances, maintaining their focus on God will ultimately lead to their deliverance.

I vividly recall a period in my life when I silently endured the anguish of domestic violence. During this time, I was concurrently supporting a colleague who was facing a similar situation. As I worked to empower her and facilitate her escape from the abusive relationship, I often found myself pondering the question of who would help me. I remember talking quite a few times with my best friend about the situation because I could not find the words to let my family know what was happening. I knew that they would not handle the news well. Despite the immense challenges that I faced, I made a conscious effort to present myself with a composed demeanor, concealing the turmoil that I was experiencing. For years, I walked around carrying the weight of untold struggles, but I refused to let my circumstances define me. I felt like I was living a recurring nightmare, but I knew I had the strength to overcome it. To look at me, you would have never guessed that I was going through such a challenging time. However, although I wore a brave face, I was secretly fighting to reclaim my inner light. My self-esteem had taken a hit, but I was determined to rise above the negative voices that sought to bring me down. It was a struggle to look in the mirror, but I knew that I was more than the hurtful words that he had spoken over me.

Despite what I was going through, I would engage in conversation with my colleague to ensure her well-being and that of her children. One day, she approached me and expressed her profound gratitude. She revealed that my support had been instrumental in her decision to leave the abusive relationship, stating that my actions had instilled in her the strength and courage to seek freedom. This poignant moment served as a catalyst for my own liberation, as I realized that if I could empower someone else to break free from the shackles of domestic violence, I, too, could overcome my own struggles and emerge victorious.

I recall a transformative night when I returned home from work, and I'm not sure if it was my tone or words, but it always seemed to escalate into a fight. If the food wasn't to his liking, he'd throw it on the floor, and if it was too hot or not warm enough, another fight would ensue. On this particular night, he was upset and decided to chase me with a hammer. I was exhausted from the constant fighting, so I made a bold decision to stop running and confront him. I told him that if he was going to harm me, I'd rather he do it then and there because I refused to continue fighting. I had no fight left in me, so I sat outside on the steps, waiting for him to strike me in the head. My neighbor ran out, crying and screaming, asking why this was happening. I told her I was tired of fighting, and she begged him not to hurt me, saying I didn't deserve such treatment.

In that moment, something shifted inside me. I realized that if my neighbor could cry for me, then there was still hope. I had my children to live for, and I knew I had to be strong for them. So, I went back inside, and when he hit me, something went all over me, and I snapped. I found the strength to fight back, and I stood up for myself. It was a turning point for me, and I knew that I would never go back to living in fear. I told myself that I was done with fighting, and I never wanted my children to think that this was what life was about. If this was love, I definitely didn't want it. So, I made a vow to myself that night that I would never live like this again, and I'm proud to say that I've kept that promise.

At this pivotal moment in my life, I discovered that God had an extraordinary plan for me, and it was truly a transformative experience that ignited my passion to empower others to overcome adversity. I embarked on a journey to pursue a career that would enable me to make a profound impact, and I found my true calling in the healthcare industry. I am deeply passionate about helping others, and my years of service in home healthcare, caring for those who could not care for themselves, was the most rewarding decision I ever made. One thing I can confidently say is that healthcare is not for everyone, but it is undoubtedly my divine purpose! The feeling of just knowing that my presence alone can brighten up someone else's day is truly uplifting. The joy of being able to truly use what has happened to me to push others through is truly a blessing. I decided to end my journey with working in the Home Health Care field after 4 years and start my journey as a CNA (certified nursing assistant) for years in a skilled nursing facility.

The work was hard, but I was dedicated to helping those who were in need of my help. At this point, it wasn't about telling my story but more about what I could do to help those around me who needed my help. By spending time with individuals who rely on others for everyday tasks like brushing their teeth or taking a bath, we can ignite a profound sense of gratitude and compassion that transforms our lives. Embracing opportunities to uplift others can be a life-changing experience that fuels positive growth, renewal, and empowerment.

As a CST II, I'm honored to empower individuals to overcome life's obstacles, igniting my passion to leverage my expertise in inspiring others during their darkest moments. I'm also grateful to provide a compassionate, listening presence that cultivates resilience, hope, and transformation.

From Pain to Purpose: My Journey to Empower and Heal

Since I can remember, I have had a heart to help others. I can remember my sister telling me a few times that if and when I came into a lot of money, she would have to take over because I would just give it all away and needed to learn how to say no. And yes, my sister doesn't have a problem saying no! I'm just truly grateful for all that I had to endure and all that I had to overcome.

But one thing is for sure: if I had to go through it all over again to be able to help and pull others out, I would choose the same road because everything that I had to go through made me the strong person that I am today. Everything that I had to go through taught me so much. I now know my worth, that I am a queen, and that I deserve nothing but the finer things in life. I am passionate about empowering young adults to reach their full potential and recognize their worth. I have made mistakes, but I refuse to let my past define me. Instead, I remind myself daily that I am capable of overcoming any obstacle that attempts to hinder my divine purpose. I express gratitude to God every day for guiding me on my journey, keeping me safe and healthy, and allowing me to uplift and inspire others.

Many of us may have endured and suffered from domestic violence in silence due to the fear of uncertainty and the potential judgment of others. It's truly remarkable how easily people can offer their opinions on what one should or shouldn't do without fully understanding the struggles of trying to save not only your life but also the lives of those you love. It's a difficult concept to grasp unless you've had to fear for your life and develop a precise escape plan. Let's never underestimate the mental state of others, as we're all too aware that some haven't survived, but I'm eternally grateful that God spared my life and the lives of my children.

As we take a step back, we realize that our shared human experience is rooted in emotions. It's not easy to navigate, however. At first, I struggled to comprehend why I had to endure so much. The battles with domestic violence, depression, and anxiety felt overwhelming, and for a long time, I carried the weight of my past in silence. But as I began to open up, I realized something powerful—my experiences were not in vain. God was using my story to help others find their way out, just as He delivered me. But for those of us who have climbed mountains, don't hide your story, as it's time to inspire those silently suffering.

I've come to understand that my journey—though marked by pain, guilt, and uncertainty—was never meant to break me. Instead, it equipped me to walk alongside other women on their own paths toward healing, freedom, and restoration.

Because of His grace and my healing, I now stand as an Accredited Certified Life Recovery Coach, Mental Health Specialist, Christian Counselor, and Certified Trauma Informed Coach equipped not only with knowledge but also with real, lived experience. I don't just understand what these women are going through—I see them, hear them, and walk with them toward the life they deserve.

Out of this purpose, Lady Shannel Coaching and Consulting LLC was born. At Lady Shannel Coaching and Consulting LLC, we are committed to:

- Helping women escape domestic violence safely
- Providing the tools to heal from trauma and break free from emotional bondage
- Restoring confidence, self-love, and self-respect
- Teaching women how to properly forgive themselves and their abusers so they can move forward without guilt or shame
- Encouraging women to build a life of peace, love, joy, and happiness—one that they never have to recover from.

Sisters, you are NOT alone. Your past does not define you, and your pain is NOT the end of your story. You can heal. You can thrive. You can reclaim your life. And I am here to walk that journey with you.

If you or someone you know needs support, reach out. Your new beginning starts today.

I am deeply inspired by my sister, who transformed every obstacle into an opportunity, refusing to let her experiences hold her back. My sister is my real-life hero, embodying the strength and resilience that defines a remarkable woman. As the saying goes, never judge a book by its cover; that is truly my sister! What happens when resilience and strength become the guiding forces in your life? For years, my sister embodied the power of perseverance, transforming the pain that could have defeated many into a beacon of hope, inspiring women everywhere to rise above and empower themselves daily. My sister, an extraordinary example of resilience, has skillfully transformed her life experiences into a catalyst for growth, emerging stronger, more determined, and purpose-driven. She has risen above adversity, reframed her mindset, and is now building a lasting legacy that will inspire and empower future generations.

My sister is a shining example of courage and compassion, inspiring me in countless ways. At a remarkably young age, she showed extraordinary resilience in the face of adversity, selflessly caring for her husband after a near-fatal shooting. Her unwavering commitment to her vows and her role in guiding her husband back to health despite overwhelming challenges is a testament to the transformative power of love and devotion. Her journey is a powerful symbol of hope, illuminating the potential for growth, transformation, and resilience in the face of hardship. I'm sure many of you would have considered a skilled nursing facility, given the challenges of caregiving at that age, but my sister's journey took a remarkable turn, revealing God's extraordinary plan for her and inspiring me to recognize her as my forever hero!

Just in case you're still trying to understand why my sister is my real-life hero, let me walk you through just one day in her world—one that is anything but ordinary. My sister and her late husband welcomed their first child, my niece, at just 16 years old. By the age of 21, they were married, building a life together. But in December of that same year, just five days before Christmas, their world shattered. What began as a typical day turned into a nightmare when her husband became the victim of a violent robbery. He was shot more than five times and left for dead. He survived, but the injuries left him paralyzed from the neck down, entirely dependent on life-sustaining medical devices and constant physical assistance. Faced with an unimaginable reality, my sister made a choice that few young women would even consider—she refused to place him in a skilled nursing facility, instead choosing to care for him at home.

She put her life on hold to keep her family together, ensuring that their daughter could bond with her father, giving him more time to cherish the little girl who was the apple of his eye. It was an act of selflessness, resilience, and love so deep that it defied the odds. How many young women do you know who would put their own dreams and ambitions aside to prioritize the care of their spouse?

My sister did—and that's why she is, and always will be, my hero. In fact, to know my sister is to absolutely adore her, and I'm not just saying that because she's my sister; I'm saying it because anyone can say 'I do,' but not everyone can rise to the challenge of caring for someone who requires 24/7 care, 365 days a year. For 7 and half years, she did this with very limited help from the nurses that she was supposed to have because they barely showed up for their shifts. She had to be his rock, his guiding light, and his everything, and it takes a truly special person to honor their wedding vows so selflessly. But what's truly remarkable is that she didn't just meet this challenge; she exceeded it with love, compassion, and dedication. Not once did she complain; instead, she took the cards she was dealt and played them with courage, resilience, and devotion until his very last breath.

You know how the saying goes: Give your loved ones their flowers while they are here on earth. All I can say is that the flowers blossomed into a beautiful garden. And in my eyes, that's the true meaning of dedication, especially at such a young age. How many people can honestly say they could handle that kind of responsibility with such grace and humility? And to be honest, there are not too many older people who would take on such a big responsibility. Although my sister may stand at 4'10, she's small in body but big in stature. I often remind her of how incredibly proud I am of her because she bravely defied the odds and proved many doubters wrong.

The majority of people who were so quick to judge and turn their noses up were left in awe; even the doctors were impressed. If and when he had to go for a doctor's appointment, the nurses were always so excited to see them and would always tell her that he was one of the best patients they had and that they loved how he was well-taken care of. They never had anything to worry about when they came for their appointments, and to be honest, because of who my sister is, I'm sure that even at appointments, she still did everything for him. One thing is for certain, two things for sure: she endured many sleepless nights, and I'm sure there were days when she shed many tears, but remarkably, when asked if she would choose a different path, her response is always a resounding NO without any hesitation. You never know how strong you can be until you're faced with a tragedy, and although the wind was knocked completely out of my sister, truly, she was bent but never broken. As her little big sister, I feel like I need to constantly remind her of her amazing strength and just how DOPE she really is because what she had to endure was truly mind-blowing. She is and has always been such a humble and selfless person who does so much for others behind closed doors. Her inspiring story and testimony have resonated with people worldwide, and if you haven't discovered her empowering book Pain Equals Purpose, you're missing out on a transformative experience.

This remarkable book has uplifted both women and men, reminding us that true love endures life's challenges and triumphs, and that's the kind of partnership we should all strive for. My Apostle used to tell us all the time, "Marry your soulmate, not your jail mate."

Now that I have your full attention, I'd like to share another awe-inspiring reason why LRW is my ultimate hero and role model. Not only is she an incredibly gifted and stunning individual, but she's also a phenomenal 10-time bestselling author, internationally acclaimed speaker, and devoted community leader who embodies the essence of selflessness. With a plethora of prestigious awards and accolades, including three esteemed Presidential Lifetime Achievement Awards, LRW continues to leave an indelible mark on humanity. Her remarkable personal journey, marked by unwavering resilience and unrelenting determination, has led her to discover her true purpose in life—empowering others. Through her enlightening podcast, 'All Bets On Me,' LRW shares her powerful voice and inspiring story, educating and empowering others to create transformative positive change by betting on themselves! By sharing her own story, she empowers others to do the same, igniting a transformative movement of resilience and triumph over adversity. Clearly, her unwavering strength and faith have shown that even in the darkest moments, a brighter future is possible, inspiring others to tap into their own inner resilience and trust that they, too, can overcome.

The Bible tells us in Proverbs 3:6 KJV not to lean on our own understanding: "In all thy ways acknowledge him, And he shall direct thy paths." You see, LRW was unaware of God's plans for her, but she was certain about the intensity of her pain and the reality of her struggle.

Even when the reasons behind our circumstances elude us, we must persist in trusting a power greater than ourselves. The Bible never promised an easy journey, and indeed, the path was fraught with obstacles and unexpected challenges. Yet, my sister continued to look toward the hills, unwavering in her conviction that her strength was derived from the Lord.

As I conclude, I hope you'll take away a powerful message: never underestimate your capabilities until you've tried, and don't let others discourage you from pursuing your passions. My sister's journey is a testament to this. If she had listened to the naysayers, she wouldn't have been able to bring her husband home and create a lifelong bond between her daughter and father. Though her father may be at rest in heaven, his memory will remain etched in his daughter's heart forever. In times of longing, they can find comfort in knowing he's watching over them. Life's unpredictability can be overwhelming, but it's essential to remember that you're not alone. You have the support of loved ones and the guidance of a higher power, empowering you to navigate life's challenges with courage and resilience. By embracing this mindset, you can rise above adversity and uncover opportunities for growth and transformation. Indeed, our brokenness can be a catalyst for transformation, and that's why my sister and I have emerged from our struggles as stronger, wiser, and more resilient individuals. We were once Broken but are now Brilliant!

FROM BROKENNESS TO BRILLIANCE

ABOUT THE AUTHOR

DAWANNA S. ALEXANDER

Dawanna S. Alexander is the CEO and Founder of Lady Shannel Coaching and Consulting LLC and CEO of Real Talk With Lady Shannel Podcast. Dawanna is an Accredited and Certificated Life Recovery Coach, Mental Health Specialist, Christian Counselor, and Certified Trauma Informed Coach.

Dawanna's most recent noteworthy accomplishments include being an international motivational speaker and an international best-selling author.

Through many trials and tribulations, Dawanna has gained strength and developed a passion for helping others bounce back from life's setbacks. Her passion for helping and serving others doesn't end there. In her current role as a CST II with UNC Hospital, Dawanna is able to walk in her purpose and do what she loves to do.

Dawanna feels that motivating and encouraging others brings new meaning to life as she loves to push others to their NEXT LEVEL through her unique coaching programs.

Dawanna is a dedicated Woman of God, wife, and mother. Dawanna is a proud member of Deliverance Through Christ Outreach Ministry, located in Pittsboro, North Carolina.

Aside from this, she is very family-oriented and loves spending time with family and friends. Most importantly, she is a true WOG who truly loves the Lord. Life has taught her that although she may bend, she will not break. She shall not be defeated.

Connect with Dawanna on Social Media through her Facebook and Instagram Business page at Lady Shannel Coaching and Consulting, LLC.
- Email: ladyshannel81@gmail.com
- Phone: (743) 208-4738

CHAPTER 6

CULTIVATING PASSION AND CONFIDENCE:
Rebuilding Self-Esteem and Rediscovering Joy

By Dr. Karon Graves

"I can do all things through Christ which strengtheneth me."
Philippians 4:13

Every challenge I've faced has shaped the person I am becoming. Pain is not the end but a stepping stone to growth. Though I've struggled, my struggles have not defined me. The old saying, "Sticks and stones may break my bones, but words will never hurt me," raises an essential question: How much power do we give to the words of others? And perhaps more importantly, what do we say to ourselves?

Proverbs 18:21 declares, "The power of life and death is in the tongue." This profound truth reminds us that words hold immense power—the power to create or destroy, uplift or tear down. Do we truly believe this? How do the influences of nature and nurture shape how we internalize what others say about us? How have our perceptions and experiences impacted our self-esteem?

I carried the weight of my past, allowing old wounds and harmful words to shape my thoughts, behaviors, and beliefs. But at some point, I realized that to heal and grow, I had to change how I thought about myself, the words I spoke, the reactions and behaviors I exhibited, and the beliefs I held onto so tightly. I was becoming my worst enemy. I desperately needed to change, and it required self-reflection, intentional effort, and a commitment to becoming the best version of myself. I had to unlearn patterns that no longer served me and replace them with habits that would nurture my growth. "Therefore, since we are surrounded by such a huge crowd of witnesses to the life of faith, let us strip off every weight that slows us down, especially the sin that so easily trips us up. And let us run with endurance the race God has set before us" (Hebrews 12:1). This scripture is a reminder that I cannot live the life promised until I can let go of my past.

Although we all experience pain, it is not our destination.

Early Memories That Shaped Me

Some memories leave deep imprints on our hearts and minds, shaping how we see ourselves and the world around us. One memory that stands out is from when I was around six or seven years old. I came home from school upset and crying because my classmates had mocked me. They teased my hair, laughing at the way my two braids stuck out, comparing me to Pippi Longstocking. They also pointed out my clothing, features, and the gap in my teeth, adding to my feelings of self-consciousness.

At the time, it felt unbearable. Their laughter chipped away at my sense of self-worth, planting seeds of self-doubt that would grow as I encountered similar experiences throughout my childhood. Looking back now, I can laugh at the innocence of it all, but at that moment, it was anything but funny. Children can be cruel without realizing the long-lasting effects of their words.

Over time, those small, hurtful moments compounded. It wasn't just my peers' words that affected me—it was also the criticism I received at home. Constant remarks about my weight chipped away at my confidence, while the harsh discipline I endured further eroded my sense of self-worth. Imagine being a child offered an entirely new wardrobe—but only if you lost weight—as though your value was tied solely to your appearance. Imagine feeling so self-conscious that you couldn't leave the house unless every hair was perfectly in place, desperately striving to meet an impossible standard of acceptance.

Now, imagine being just 10 years old, your body developing far too soon, drawing the inappropriate attention of grown men who whistled as you walked down the street. Imagine the heartbreak and betrayal of being inappropriately touched by someone you trusted, like a church deacon, leaving you confused, ashamed, and silent. I battled thoughts no child should ever face, including the overwhelming despair of contemplating suicide. Imagine growing up in a home where domestic violence and alcohol abuse were part of daily life, only to realize those patterns would haunt you into adulthood.

Imagine feeling the sting of rejection at every turn, as though no matter how hard you tried, you could never be good enough. Imagine the pain of going through a divorce, leaving behind family, friends, and a tenured career—all in a desperate attempt to escape the very pain you had spent a lifetime trying to overcome, only to face it again in unfamiliar ways.

A Defining Encounter

One encounter with my father stands out vividly as a pivotal moment in my life. I was about nine or ten years old. He accused me of stealing money he had hidden under the carpet in his room. His anger was palpable—his bloodshot eyes and harsh words revealed a rage I could neither understand nor escape.

Despite my tearful denials, he was unrelenting. I remember the sound of his belt buckle jingling as he stormed toward me, and I braced myself for the punishment I knew was coming. The pain of the beating was excruciating, but the emotional scars it left behind cut even deeper. I prayed for relief, for it all to stop. When it finally did, I climbed out of my bedroom window and walked to my aunt's house, seeking refuge.

Later that night, my parents came to bring me home. My mother explained that my father had found the missing money—it had merely shifted further under the carpet. This would not be the last time I would pack up and leave home due to the physical discipline of my father. Though he apologized years later, the damage was already done, and in these later years, hearing him say, "I love you" still leaves a numbing effect. That experience shattered my trust in him and left a lasting impact on how I viewed future relationships, especially with men.

The Role of Parents in Shaping Self-Worth

Parents are a child's first love. A father sets the foundation for his daughter's sense of worth, teaching her how she should be treated by others. A mother, on the other hand, should be her role model and greatest supporter. When those roles falter, the effects can be profound and long-lasting.

In my case, the breakdown of these foundational relationships left me grappling with questions about my self-worth for decades. My father's harsh words and actions left me feeling broken and unworthy, and my mother's silence often made me feel unsupported. Together, these experiences shaped how I interacted with the world and how I allowed others to treat me. However, time and healing have led to forgiveness.

I promised myself that this generational marker would not be passed down to my children, and with determination, I would foster a life for my children filled with opportunities and experiences that would promote their growth. Additionally, expressing my love would be built into my daily routine, letting them know how much I love them. My desire was that my pain would not be passed on.

The Shift: Choosing Resilience

> *"I can do all things through Christ which strengtheneth me."*
> *Philippians 4:13*

For years, I carried the heavy emotional and physical weight of my past—so much so that my weight eventually exceeded 300 pounds, leading to the onset of medical issues. In my mid-30s, I discovered high blood pressure and lumps in my left breast. The fear that gripped me in that moment was overwhelming as my mind raced with thoughts of the worst possible outcomes.

That experience became my wake-up call. I realized I needed to fight for my life, not just for myself but for the sake of my children. My longevity, my future, and my ability to be present for them were suddenly in question. I knew I couldn't continue down the same path—I had to change, and I had to do it quickly.

This forced me to confront hard truths and ask myself some deeply personal questions:

Do I truly believe the hurtful words others have spoken about me?

What is my honest belief about who I am at my core?

Am I ready to let go of the pain and take the first steps toward healing and growth?

These questions weren't easy to face, but they marked the beginning of my journey toward resilience, self-discovery, and reclaiming the life I deserved.

Psalm 55:22 reminds us, "Cast your burden on the Lord, and He shall sustain you." Through self-examination and a deep desire to heal, I realized that my worth was not tied to my past or the opinions of others. Instead, it was rooted in who I am as a child of God.

This realization marked the beginning of a shift in my life—a shift toward resilience, self-love, and purpose. Words of kindness, encouragement, and hope became my new language. When self-doubt crept in, I replaced it with affirmations like:

"I am strong and resilient."

"I am worthy."

"I am enough."

"I am capable of overcoming any challenge."

"I deserve love and happiness."

Steps Toward Healing and Rediscovering Joy

"He gives strength to the weary and increases the power of the weak."
Isaiah 40:29

Healing in the spiritual realm can be defined as "restoration" and "deliverance" or the process of becoming whole and healthy. It is intricately linked to the concept of "freedom," representing liberation from the chains of past pain, trauma, or unfulfilled expectations. It encompasses the entirety of who we are—our body, mind, and spirit—and requires an intentional focus on the whole person.

True healing is a lifetime journey and does not occur quickly or overnight. Along the path toward healing, we must allow ourselves grace in those moments of triggers, setbacks, and growth. These moments do not signify failure but are opportunities for deeper understanding and transformative change. This is truly a reminder that healing is a process where new insights and challenges often surface as we further develop.

I recall the disappointment I felt after my first major argument with my significant other. The intensity of that conflict brought unresolved feelings from my childhood, and my relationship with my father came rushing back to the surface. Initially, I felt as though this resurgence of pain indicated that I wasn't healed. However, I came to understand that healing doesn't mean the absence of pain or struggle; it means embracing the process of growth and acknowledging that there is always more work to be done.

Instead of praying for God to change my partner, I began asking God to change me. This shift in perspective opened the door to self-reflection and personal accountability. There were and still are moments in our relationship that test my patience and resilience, forcing me to confront and work through the deeply rooted triggers of repressed trauma and memories. These instances became building blocks for polishing my character and affirming my identity.

Through time, prayer, and perseverance, I learned to stand in my truth. I discovered the power of using my voice to set boundaries and communicate my needs while reaffirming my worth to myself. This journey taught me that healing is not just about fixing the past but also about building a stronger foundation for the future. Healing is about choosing freedom—freedom to grow, freedom to love, and freedom to embrace who you are, flaws, scars, and all. It is a reoccurring process, one that requires a commitment to faith, patience, and the willingness to face challenges with your head held high, courage, and an open heart.

But how did I get here, you might ask? Here are five tips for healing that have helped me.

1. Practice Gratitude:
Gratitude became a cornerstone of my healing journey. By focusing on the blessings in my life, I was able to shift my perspective and find joy even in the midst of pain. Gratitude opened the door to hope and allowed me to embrace life fully. The key is to live in the moment and focus on the here and now. Just being thankful for the simple things in life makes a difference. Grab a journal and just write your thoughts. Focus on the positive aspects of your life. Gratitude welcomes joy.

2. Seek Professional Help:
Therapy was a game-changer for me. It provided a safe space to unpack the pain of my past and process my emotions. Through counseling, I learned to let go of the burdens I had carried for so long and began to live more abundantly. I had to take actionable steps to align my behaviors with my new mindset. I prioritized self-care, set boundaries to protect my emotional well-being, and sought out healthy environments that nurtured growth. Instead of reacting impulsively to triggers, I practiced meditation and learned to respond

thoughtfully. This shift allowed me to take control of my emotions and break free from old patterns of behavior that kept me stuck in pain. It's okay to ask for help.

3. Forgive and Release:
Forgiveness is not about excusing the actions of others—it's about freeing yourself from the chains of resentment. Forgiving my father was one of the hardest things I've ever done, but it was also one of the most liberating. Forgiving others I trusted and loved also gave me a sense of peace. Although forgiveness does not erase experiences, it allows for a level of freedom. We just can't keep living in our pain. Forgiveness is one of the best gifts that we can ever give to ourselves.

4. Focus on the Present:
Happiness grows when you focus on the present moment rather than dwelling on the past or worrying about the future. I've found that ignoring any negativity around me and concentrating on positivity and the strength in myself and others helps me live in the moment. Mindfulness practices helped me stay grounded and appreciate the here and now. These practices include taking a body inventory, monitoring my breathing, walking, and spending time in nature.

5. Build Trusting Relationships:
I have struggled with the ability to allow people to get close to me and in friendships and relationships. The feeling of possible harm has, at times, overshadowed my connections with others. Again, this was shaped based on childhood experiences and encounters with others. It took time; however, genuine, supportive relationships became a

source of comfort and encouragement. Also, I had to ask myself if I was capable of being to others what I wanted for myself. This continues to be a work in progress and a continued area of growth. However, by surrounding myself with people who uplifted and inspired me, I was able to rebuild my trust in others and rediscover the beauty of connection. I learned that I can not expect me from other people. I learned that it does not require a large crowd or group of people.

Practical Tips for Thriving

"Do not be conformed to this world but be transformed by the renewal of your mind. Then you will be able to test what God's will is – his good, pleasing, and perfect will." –Romans 12:2-3

The term "thriving" can be described as the active pursuit of purpose, growth, development, evolution, and progress. Thriving is not about living a life devoid of hurt, disappointment, or pain; rather, it is about rising above these challenges and finding strength within ourselves. It's about embracing resilience and recognizing that even in the face of adversity, we have the power to build a meaningful and fulfilling life.

Thriving means creating a life anchored in self-love, purpose, and happiness. It involves making intentional choices to nurture our well-being and align with our values and dreams. When was the last time you reevaluated your dreams or considered your value or worth? Thriving, for me, has been about transforming every negative experience into an opportunity for growth while trying to find the positive in every experience. Each challenge I've faced has become a stepping stone, teaching me lessons, shaping my character, and empowering me to move forward with greater clarity and strength. For example, when I have been faced with a situation that I felt was unfair or motivated from a negative space, instead of arguing and fighting, I chose to be silent and instead ask God, "What do you want me to see and learn from this?"

Like healing, to thrive is to acknowledge the complexity of life while choosing to focus on what fosters joy, peace, and fulfillment. It's an ongoing process that requires patience, transparency, courage, adaptability, and a commitment to personal growth. By reframing "setbacks" to "falls forward" as opportunities and embracing the journey of self-discovery, thriving becomes not just a state of being but a way of life.

The keys to unlocking the ability to thrive begin with the following:

1. Recognize Your Value:
You are inherently worthy, regardless of your circumstances or past. Celebrate your strengths and take pride in your achievements, no matter how small. I believe that we must know our value, understand our worth, and add tax. We must value ourselves first before expecting it from others.

2. Challenge Negative Thoughts:
Replace self-doubt with affirmations of your capabilities. Speak to yourself with the same kindness and compassion you would offer a dear friend. My healing began with my thoughts. I realized that my

internal emotions were often more critical and unforgiving than the words of others. I had to confront these negative thought patterns and challenge them. Instead of focusing on my flaws, I began to affirm my strengths and capabilities. I reminded myself that I am worthy of love, respect, and happiness—regardless of my past or the opinions of others. Romans 12:2-3: "Do not be conformed to this world but be transformed by the renewal of your mind. Then you will be able to test what God's will is – his good, pleasing, and perfect will."

3. Set Achievable Goals:

Every accomplishment, no matter how minor, builds confidence and fosters self-worth. Progress happens one step at a time. I always dreamed of having my own business, and in 2022, after separating from a toxic work environment, Push Towards Purpose was born. This marked the beginning of my journey into entrepreneurship. Skills I had once buried or forgotten were reignited, coming to the forefront as I embraced this new chapter. With each step forward, I rediscovered my strengths, reignited my passion, and began building a purpose-driven life that aligned with my true self.

Moving Forward

Thriving isn't about avoiding pain—it's about rising above it. It's about rediscovering your strength, embracing joy, and choosing to create a life filled with purpose and love.

Your past doesn't define you, but your choices do. Let go of what no longer serves you and step boldly into a future of self-love and brilliance. I had spent so much of my life internalizing the opinions of others, believing I wasn't enough or that I didn't deserve happiness. It took time, but I began dismantling those limiting beliefs and replacing them with truths rooted in love and self-worth.

One belief that sustained me during this journey was: "I am not defined by what has happened to me but by how I choose to rise above it." I have the power to rewrite my story, and so do you. Our pain is a chapter in our book of life, not the whole story.

Finally, rebuilding self-esteem and rediscovering joy is not only possible but within reach for each of us. The journey to thriving begins with the courage to confront the pain and the willingness to embrace the change. It requires a deliberate effort to nurture passion and confidence, even when faced with challenges that test our strength. Cultivating passion involves reconnecting with the activities, dreams, and aspirations that ignite our inner desires. Whether through creative expression, meaningful work, or relationships that bring us joy, passion provides a sense of purpose that fuels our growth. Tap into your passion to find your purpose. It reminds us that life is not only about surviving but about finding and embracing what makes us live life fully and abundantly.

Confidence, on the other hand, is built through consistent self-affirmation and taking small, courageous steps toward our goals. Tell yourself every day that you are great, amazing, and worthy. Our confidence will grow as we honor our own achievements, no matter how small, and learn to trust our own abilities. Confidence empowers us to face the future with hope and determination, even when the road ahead feels uncertain.

Thriving beyond the pain means recognizing that my struggle, your struggle, and our struggles do not define us; instead, they shape us into stronger, more compassionate people. It's about transforming our bruises into symbols of resilience and viewing setbacks as opportunities to learn and evolve. This transformation allows us to rebuild our self-esteem on a foundation of self-love and acceptance.

Rediscovering joy is a vital part of this process. Joy is found in the simple, everyday moments—in laughter, connection, and the beauty of the world around us. It's about allowing ourselves to feel gratitude and wonder, even in times of difficulty. By embracing joy, we reclaim our true power and remind ourselves that life holds golden moments of light, no matter how uncertain or dark it may seem.

Ultimately, cultivating passion and confidence allows us to PUSH and PRESS beyond pain, turning our wounds into wisdom and our challenges into triumphs. This journey is deeply personal yet universally achievable, as we each have the capacity to rebuild, grow, and flourish into the best version of ourselves. The path to thriving may not always be easy, but it is always worth it.

Remember, you are not alone; we each have experiences that have shaped our lives and world.

Together, let's stand on our faith and the promise of being made whole. Hebrews 11:6 says, "But without faith it is impossible to please him: for he that cometh to God must believe that he is, and that he is a rewarder of them that diligently seek him."

ABOUT THE AUTHOR

DR. KARON GRAVES

Early on in her professional career, Dr. Karon Graves centered her energy around working with vulnerable populations within the community. Her passion for serving others began in Massachusetts (1991) in Early Childhood Education, where she served in various capacities, from teacher to educational resource coordinator. She continued to expand her career and spent some years working with developmentally disabled adults.

In 2002, Dr. Graves began her career in child welfare, providing direct services to children and families through the State of Connecticut Department of Children and Families. During her tenure with the State of Connecticut Department of Children and Families, she served in many social work and supervisor roles for over 13 years of service. In 2015, after relocating to North Carolina, she continued her work in child welfare, where she continues to serve with over 20 years of overall service.

Dr. Graves is an adoptive parent after fostering a relative placement for 6 years in Massachusetts. During her time serving as a relative foster parent, she became a CASA-certified Guardian Et. Lithium in an effort to advocate for timely permanency outcomes for children in the foster care system.

Dr. Karon Graves is a graduate of Springfield College, where she earned both a Bachelor of Science and a Master of Science in Human Services. She holds a PhD in Christian Leadership from the Purpose Zeal Bible College and Seminary. Her additional educational experience includes doctoral studies in counseling. Dr. Graves is a Certified Recovery Life Coach. Dr. Graves holds several other certifications related to Early Childhood Education.

Dr. Graves is the founder of Push Towards Purpose Supportive Services, LLC, a recovery life coaching company founded on the belief that everyone deserves the support and guidance needed to achieve their desired goals. Through Push Towards Purpose, she strives to help individuals who have been impacted by trauma and life stress-related challenges to make positive changes in their lives. Dr. Graves works with an experienced team of professionals who provide the best possible service to clients, ensuring that they are well-supported and have the tools and resources to work toward their goals. She is passionate about helping people find their purpose and take the necessary steps to achieve success. She is also committed to helping her clients create the life they desire and deserve.

Dr. Graves has published a Coaching Workbook to assist others along their journey.

Dr. Graves is also the founder and owner of Push Tax Solutions, where she provides tax preparation, education, and business coaching.

With over 20 years dedicated to the field of Human Services, Dr. Graves works and volunteers in her community. She continues to be of service to others to implement change. She has been active in various communities in multiple states because of her care, compassion, and dedication to humanity.

Most importantly, Dr. Graves loves the Lord. At an early age, she gave her life to the Lord and was baptized at the age of 8 years old. Her love of God, church, and family has been her guiding light. She has served in several ministerial roles over the years, including Sunday School Teacher, Praise and Worship Leader, Usher, Choir member, Women's Day Chair, Executive Director of The Food Bank, and Trustee.

CHAPTER 7
FROM SILENCE TO SIGNIFICANCE:
Reclaiming My Voice, Boldness, and Brilliance

By Carol Andrews King

"There was a war going on inside and I didn't know how I could win, but I held onto my faith and trust in God".

Silence, like many other English words, carries several meanings—some positive and some negative. From the state of abstaining from speech to avoiding the discussion of something, silence appears to be driven by one's own choice. Conversely, when speaking is prevented by exclusion, suppression, or blockades, silence appears to be driven by external factors. But when experiences of silence become the backdrop to the testimony of a life transformed, it sends a powerful message: no matter the obstacle, the devil didn't win. It's a reminder of Philippians 1:6, "He who began a good work in you will carry it on to completion until the day of Christ Jesus."

If I were to create my own definition of silence, I'd have to include the good, the bad, and the ugly parts. Not necessarily in that order. And certainly not without inviting you to sit down for a cup of tea, coffee, or soda so that I can share my story—one that might leave you speechless or prompt you to ask questions.

I can't quite remember at what age this *silence* became a thing, so I'll just go back as far as I can remember. But, first, I was the second baby girl born into my family. My dad was a young man in the Air Force, and my mom was a homemaker at the time. While I have many childhood memories, like *most* people, I don't have as many memories prior to about age 4. However, I *do* remember that during that time, my family and I were living overseas in Japan, and my big sister, who was two and a half years older, was my built-in best friend. What I didn't know *then* but would learn later was that *she* would become my childhood mouthpiece. While I was, in fact, born with the ability to verbalize, for whatever reason, I was shy, extremely quiet, and often withdrawn, never initiating a lot of conversations or volunteering to share my thoughts much. What looked like me being a quiet kid really was a ploy of the enemy to put a "muzzle over my mouth" at a young age when I was innocent, vulnerable, and unaware of who I was or would become if I got to know Jesus. Keep that in mind as you continue reading.

Living in Japan was short-lived, and my dad's military assignment brought us back statewide to Virginia at a time when being a 5-year-old kindergartner meant experiences were quite impressionable. Being 5 was fun at times—getting in trouble for climbing onto the countertop to eat spoonfuls of peanut butter right out of the jar, learning to ride a bike without training wheels, learning to skate on steel skates attached to my shoes, catching fireflies in a jar in the summertime, and eating bomb pop popsicles from the ice cream truck. Yet, there were some negative memories, too, that somehow stayed with me, and maybe, just maybe, that's where the idea of *silence* tried to set in. At least, that's the earliest that I can recall.

Besides dealing with mean kids, there were times in school when a few teachers misinterpreted my shy, quiet, and introverted nature—an assumption that followed me into adulthood. I'll get to my adulthood stories later. However, one memory in particular is quite vivid to me, from the incident to what I was wearing that day. It started off as a normal day. I was wearing my favorite outfit, an off-white long-sleeve top with brown polka dots and a pair of brown pants. I couldn't have known or guessed what the day's outcome would be as a little kid who only knew how to live in the moment, but my big sister and I rode the bus to school, and the day seemed fine.

At the end of the school day, my kindergarten teacher announced the time to prepare to go home, and she and the aide helped the students get ready for parent pick-up or to get on the bus. Some students lined up to use the restroom, while others were helped to gather their backpacks and lunch boxes. Once I realized I needed to go to the restroom, I got in line, only to be told that I should've gone earlier. I was guided out of the line and ushered outside to catch the bus with my big sister, who was waiting for me. My sister and I sat in the front right seat of the school bus. The ride seemed longer that day as I sat in a puddle of wetness in my favorite polka-dotted outfit. I felt smaller than usual, alone and belittled, even though I didn't know the definition of those words at the time.

My sister tucked her arm around me, trying to shield me from the humiliation as other kids teased me about wetting myself. I was made to be a spectacle and was deeply saddened. Something stuck with me that day: a mistrust and fear of speaking up, as though I wasn't born with a voice at all. Because of that, my first few years were challenging, and it seemed that adults were no kinder than kids when it came to pointing out the fact that I didn't say much. Thankfully, my big sister spoke up for and often fought for me, but she could only shield me so much. So, when she wasn't around, I often stood quietly, frozen and unsure. I mean, what would someone like me have to say?

By age 7, things hadn't changed much. I talked and played with my sister and friends, but overall, I remained a pretty quiet kid, which affected my confidence in social settings. Second grade was one of those times when that part of me was tested, especially with subjects that weren't my strong suit, like the times that I didn't understand the math assignments. When raising my hand and asking for help too many times became an issue, the teacher fussed at me, spanked me, and called my parents for a parent/teacher conference, further driving me away from initiating participation, even if I had the right answers. Unfortunately, this became a pattern hovering over my life, sending a message that I didn't matter, and neither did what I had to say. So, why say anything when I wouldn't be heard, anyway? Those experiences continued throughout elementary school, at a time when not only did I feel God calling me to salvation, but I also sensed, even as young as age 8, that He wanted to use me in some great ways that I didn't understand yet. But how could God use someone like me, who is not only shy, introverted, and extremely quiet but who struggled with thoughts of being insignificant? Time and time again, I was subjected to the idea of not being good enough.

By junior high school (7th and 8th grade), I really struggled to figure out who I was while, at the same time, trying to overcome rejection. I was rejected by several people, while others, who appeared to have it all together in looks, popularity, and the ability to naturally lead, were chosen. Yet, I knew I had something valuable to say and offer as a person, friend, and student. But that didn't seem to matter except to my few close friends. While in 8th grade, I pondered what I wanted my life to be like. I wanted to be given opportunities, but that meant facing my biggest challenge: to speak up and speak out and to do it with confidence. This was important to me, especially since I was looking forward to becoming a 9th grader and being considered a leader in my last year on the junior high campus. How could I be a good leader if I couldn't even speak up? I made up my mind that I was going to try to start speaking up and get involved in activities that required more social interaction and leadership. So, one of the first things I did was join the yearbook club. Even as a band member, when fundraising came around, I was driven to get out into the neighborhood to sell products so that I could earn prizes and money. Those moments of placing 1st and 2nd in sales and winning those prizes and money were the catalyst for getting me on the road toward something I didn't realize was potential.

My first year of high school was 10th grade in my hometown in NC. By this time, I had learned how to canvas the neighborhood in search of babysitting gigs, which again required going door to door alone, speaking confidently to present myself as a responsible teen offering childcare services. In my eyes, it was successful. Yet, I still had moments of uncertainty where I doubted my abilities.

There was a war going on inside, and I didn't know how I could win. On the one hand, I was shy, introverted, insecure, and uncertain of who I really was. On the other hand, I had an inner drive to break out of the shell I was in. I didn't like the shell and was desperate to outgrow it, shed it altogether, and leave it behind, but it stayed stuck onto me, something not easy to be loosened. Thankfully, my big sister was a great role model in letting *her* voice be known. I had been a quiet, unofficial student of hers since day one. I wanted to be like her because, in my opinion, she was the essence of confidence, unafraid to speak her mind. So, when I entered high school, I followed in her footsteps, thinking it would help me break free. I signed up for drama class, the same one she had taken a few years before. However, some very significant experiences impacted my life in both negative and positive ways. Even though my mind was set on making life changes, I failed to realize that my natural personality was very much a part of who I was and that it wouldn't change overnight.

So, when my first drama class assignment was due, thoughts of insignificance, uncertainty, and fear took over completely, and I was given a zero for not completing it. Not only did the conversation with my teacher and parents affect me, but their disappointment in me and my disappointment in myself attempted to drown me into deeper thoughts that maybe what everyone had been saying about me was true all along. Maybe the treatment I endured was valid. Then, to make matters worse, I forgot part of my speech while at the church's young program and endured kids' laughs when the curtain opened with me standing with my props, as my voice remained silent. Thankfully, the same year, a positive experience took place when I did a presentation at school that progressed me to the regional competition, and while at the out-of-town event, my parents showed up to surprise and congratulate me. Maybe that would be a turning point, but although taking the class was a good decision and I made progress speaking in front of audiences, it appeared not to be enough to leave *silence* behind.

After my first year of high school as a 10th grader, my dad's next military assignment took us across the country to Texas, far away from the family and friends I knew. I rejected the idea of moving, starting over, and leaving the life I knew, as well as the life and personality I had begun cultivating. But my pleas to stay behind fell on deaf ears. It wouldn't have made sense to be separated from my parents and 8-year-old little sister. Not only that, but it would be the first time my big sister (my childhood mouthpiece) and I would be apart, which was eating me up inside. I couldn't imagine being on my own to fend for or speak up for myself, and yet, there I was at a crossroads in life, one that I wasn't ready to face. The move thrust me into an environment in which I was forced to try to adapt, but where I felt myself struggling inwardly, my voice dwindled again, yet I didn't realize that God was working behind the scenes.

I was now a junior in a new high school and didn't really know anyone except a few kids who attended the same church my family and I attended. I spent a lot of time wishing for friendships, trying to find my place, self-searching, and learning how to thrive on what I felt was shaky ground. It was tough, and I was concerned about whether I would thrive at all or waste away in the shadows. But something inside of me wanted to live. I had an inner drive, a *quiet* one, but a drive nonetheless. Getting my first job in the real world at a local cafeteria was another avenue that taught me the importance of interacting with people.

Even though I was still naturally shy, I found myself able to fall back on what I learned in drama class: treat each moment like a stage performance, take a deep breath, then speak, and I loved it! Experiencing those moments gave me a rush, the same kind I felt back in the 10th grade, and what made it even better was my involvement in my vocational office education class at school and being a member of the Office Education Association, which instilled leadership skills. It meant staying in my shell was not an option, although being introverted was still very much a part of me.

Times moved on, experiences came and went, and struggles showed up. Still, God was with me, even during the time I met a young man at work who I began dating. I didn't know at the time how significant that relationship would be and what lessons I would learn until they presented themselves in some of the most challenging ways I had ever experienced. I had been a Christian for four years when I became pregnant at age 17. In spite of my sin, I repented. However, what I thought would be fond memories with the young man I loved ultimately turned into a nightmare where I was rejected and ostracized. Just when I thought I was getting my footing, the bottom began to fall out from under me, and the humiliation I faced during my senior year was almost too much to bear, yet I somehow made it. Though shunned and talked about openly by him and others, I never said a word. Silence was my go-to, and it fit perfectly in this situation. We were young and foolish, but things turned around in our relationship.

A year and a half later, I secretly married him, but it didn't take long for my world to fall apart and for me to feel beaten down in ways I would've never imagined. I thought I didn't have a voice and believed the things I endured were meant to destroy me. The enemy, the devil, had a field day and used the strained relationship as a way to place another muzzle over my mouth. I stayed silent a lot, keeping my troubles to myself until I couldn't stay silent anymore. I wasn't living right at all, but God's presence was with me during times I didn't understand or want Him to be. This is his reminder of Jeremiah 29:11: "For I know the plans I have for you," says the Lord, "plans to prosper you and not to harm you, plans to give you hope and a future." Remembering that scripture and my will to live took me to a new level in God and what He could do, but it took time, a lot of work, and learning how to walk away from pain to experience peace. I desperately wanted to break free from what seemed to be a voiceless life, but the devil didn't quit.

As an adult, it seemed that this dark cloud of silence was inevitable, and being mistreated or overlooked would resurface again and again. I was overlooked in different ways, and when I did get a certain position, especially in leadership, some said I was too serious or were critical in some other way. Then, there were times when I seemed to be the last resort, like an afterthought, because everyone else had been chosen. Nevertheless, I never gave up hope because a little voice inside of me was pushing me forward. However, whether as a kid or a young adult, those experiences caused me to be mistrusting and sometimes afraid to speak up, even when what I had to say was confirmed. People made negative comments, sometimes directly to me or in my vicinity, and I wouldn't say anything. It wasn't that I was okay with what they said, but rather that I didn't know what to say or how to say it. So, in my 20s, I began to wonder what life ahead would look like if only I could break out of my shell. I continued trying different methods of placing myself into situations that would require and encourage me to use my voice to make an impact, only to do well in a moment and then fall off down the road in some cases. The inconsistency almost drove me insane because I wondered if I'd ever be able to launch out and be and do great things, the things I felt in my spirit that I was called to do. The struggle was real.

By my early 30s, I had been in positions requiring public service, being a customer service worker in a grocery store and a teller for a prominent motor bank. I had also been in sales with Amway, Mary Kay, and Tupperware. I had even done well on speeches and presentations for my college classes, increasing my experience and exposure to speaking through church events. Looking back, God began to help me realize that the enemy was at work from day one to stifle my abilities through negative experiences, personal attacks, and my own self-sabotage. But it was then that God started opening my eyes. I began to better understand spiritual warfare and what it can look like, designed to keep a believer's purpose from coming to pass. My relationship with God and my commitment to studying the scriptures was the vice I needed to ponder over what God already said about me, consider what He was doing in me, and work strategically to overcome all the subtle and overt ways the devil was trying to hold me back.

Life as someone trying to find her voice seemed to throw me for a loop. The inner struggle was real. There were days that I gave the appearance of outer confidence when inside, I was still that unsure little girl who believed that others were judging me, negatively speaking over, against, or to me, hoping I would fail, or wishing I would move aside to allow someone better to come along. Then, I had some really amazing moments that appeared to prove that I *do* have a voice. God reminded me that having a voice and speaking up can have different meanings for different people: protection of oneself, creating boundaries, offering valuable insight, advocacy, and making a positive impact or change. For me, my natural abilities began to blossom and show up more in my relationships, church involvement, and career because I listened to God's voice over the enemy, naysayers, and even my own thoughts.

The Lord brought back my remembrance of how much what I was doing and was led to do was aligning with my purpose and God's will for my life. So, it began to make more sense that the devil would use different tactics and all avenues to attempt to strip me of my voice because everything I'd been called to do was directly aligned with using my voice to instruct, teach, exhort, minister, write, pray, and praise! My calling in my career as a speech-language pathologist in public schools requires my voice. To teach in women's ministry requires my voice. To exhort and empower others for greatness by sharing wisdom and knowledge requires my voice. To minister the Word of God and be fervent in intercessory prayer requires my voice. To be a public speaker in the community and at women's conferences requires my voice. To be a support group facilitator requires my voice. To write and be awarded grants for therapy materials requires my voice. To become a #1 best-selling author requires my voice. And to continue to share my stories, tell my truth, and articulate all that God has done for me requires my voice. I won't be silent anymore!

Everyone's story may not be like mine, but imagine the impact one can make when you take back your voice and power within, cultivate your inner strength in the Lord, and begin walking in your calling. You, too, can go from a life of silence to significance with God's help.

…

ABOUT THE AUTHOR

CAROL ANDREWS KING

Carol Andrews King wears different hats to fulfill her God-given destiny. Her journey from silence to significance has launched her into self-discovery, inner healing, and renewed purpose. Finding her voice has allowed her to align with God's calling in education as an assistant speech-language pathologist, as well as in women's ministry, public speaking, intercessory prayer, authorship, and becoming a certified life recovery coach.

Faith and family are first in Carol's life. She is passionate about her relationship with God, which is the foundation of everything she is and does. She listens intently to God's voice, which teaches her to speak up and speak out, to intentionally be in the will of God, and to pave the way for others, especially her adult son. She looks to purposely inspire, exhort, and impact those she meets along the way.

As a 20-year cancer survivor and someone with kidney disease, Carol knows what it means to pray fervently and with expectation so that she sets an example of Godly commitment and so that her purpose might be fulfilled for such a time as this. By sharing her story, she encourages others to realize their potential and significance when they align with their own calling(s).

You can connect with Carol on Facebook, Instagram, or LinkedIn at Carol Andrews King or by email at carolkingsbiz@gmail.com.

CHAPTER 8

FROM BROKENNESS TO BRILLIANCE:
The Power of Community and Walking in Purpose

By Dr. Lashonda Wofford

"Brokenness isn't the end—it's the beginning of something beautiful.
- Dr. Lashonda Wofford

The Power of Community Focus: Healing Together

When life brings unimaginable pain, it's easy to feel isolated, as though no one could possibly understand the weight of your burdens. But healing doesn't happen in a vacuum. It's within community—true, authentic, and supportive relationships—that we find the strength to rebuild and thrive. My journey has taught me the immeasurable value of community and, unfortunately, the pain of toxic connections as well.

I became a mother at just 16 years old. In that season, I learned quickly that support was critical but also scarce. Some people in my circle judged me harshly for my situation, while others offered a helping hand. The friends who encouraged me to keep going, who didn't see me as a statistic but as a young woman capable of rising above her circumstances, became my lifeline. Their belief in me planted the seeds of resilience that I would lean on for years to come.

When I married at 21, I was ready to create a new chapter for myself. Just four months into our marriage, life handed me an unexpected and heavy cross to bear. My husband became gravely ill, and I stepped into the role of full-time caregiver while still parenting my 5-year-old daughter. Those early days were lonely. I cried in the shower so no one could hear, and I prayed endlessly for strength. During this time, I realized not all family and friends were truly there for me. Some disappeared, unable or unwilling to deal with the weight of my reality. But others showed up in ways I'll never forget—dropping off meals, offering to babysit, or simply being a listening ear. Their kindness became my refuge.

My daughter's father's tragedy brought another layer to my understanding of community. At 21 years old, his life was changed forever when a senseless robbery left him ventilator-dependent, a quadriplegic reliant on others for his every need. I became his primary caregiver, navigating a world of medical decisions, late-night emergencies, and emotional pain. For seven and a half years, I cared for him until his passing. While some family members supported me during this time, others resented the decisions I made to protect and prioritize him. The tension was palpable, but I focused on those who stood by me, understanding the weight of my responsibility and lifting me up when I felt I couldn't go on.

One of the hardest lessons I've learned is that not everyone in your circle is in your corner. Over the past year and a half, I've faced betrayal from family members I've known my entire life. Lies, character attacks, court battles, and attempts to destroy my business have tested my resolve.

Aunts, uncles, and cousins who once laughed with me now drag my name through the mud, fueled by jealousy and envy. Their hatred has been painful, but it's also taught me the importance of letting go of toxic relationships and focusing on building a community that uplifts and supports.

In contrast, the sisterhoods I've formed through shared experiences have been my saving grace. Women who've walked similar paths, who understand the weight of caregiving, betrayal, or starting over, have become my safe space. We've laughed, cried, and encouraged each other to keep moving forward. These relationships have shown me that healing happens in the company of those who truly see you.

One of the most devastating moments in my life came when I discovered that my daughter had been repeatedly sexually violated as a child. It happened right under my nose, and the pain rippled through my entire being. I felt like I had failed her, and rage overtook me. I wanted justice, revenge, and to shield her from the world all at once.

It wasn't until I surrendered my pain to God that true healing began. He showed me how to turn that anguish into purpose and passion, to advocate for others, and to create a space where survivors can find hope and restoration. That pain, though unimaginable, birthed a mission in me to protect and empower others.

If you're on a journey of healing, I encourage you to take stock of your community. Surround yourself with people who build you up, challenge you to grow, and celebrate your victories. Let go of those who drain your spirit and make room for the connections that bring light into your life.

Again, when life brings unimaginable pain, isolation often feels like the easiest option. But healing doesn't happen in a vacuum—it happens in community. Surrounding yourself with authentic, supportive relationships is one of the most powerful ways to rebuild and thrive.

Tips and Tools for Building a Supportive Community:

1. **Identify Your Inner Circle:** Make a list of people who uplift, encourage, and challenge you to be better. These are the individuals you should lean on during tough times.
2. **Join Support Groups:** Whether online or in-person, find groups centered around shared experiences. Support groups for caregivers, survivors, or those navigating similar journeys can be life-changing.
3. **Set Boundaries:** Learn to identify toxic relationships and create boundaries to protect your mental and emotional health.

4. **Be Vulnerable:** Healing begins when we allow ourselves to be seen. Share your struggles with those you trust—it can deepen connections and open doors to unexpected support.
5. **Give Back:** When you feel strong enough, consider mentoring or supporting someone else. Helping others can be incredibly healing for both parties.

Reflection Exercise: Write down the names of 3-5 people who have positively impacted your life and consider reaching out to express your gratitude. Then, make a list of qualities you value in a supportive community, and seek to nurture those qualities in your relationships.

> "Community isn't just a place; it's the people who remind you of your strength."- Dr. Lashonda Wofford

Walking in Brilliance Focus: Living in Your Purpose

Walking in brilliance means stepping boldly into the purpose God has designed for your life despite the doubts, fears, and obstacles that may try to hold you back. It's a journey of faith, resilience, and self-discovery, and I've had to learn to embrace it fully.

At 16, when I became a mother, the idea of living a brilliant life felt unattainable. Society's expectations for young mothers were low, and I often felt the weight of judgment. But in the quiet moments, as I held my daughter in my arms, I knew there was more for me. I didn't just want to survive—I wanted to thrive, to create a life for her that was full of possibilities.

At 21, when I became a full-time caregiver to my husband, I questioned whether my dreams were still possible. Caregiving was all-consuming, and the pressure to be everything for everyone left little room for me to focus on myself. But I learned that walking in brilliance doesn't mean having everything figured out. It's about showing up each day with intention and faith, even when the path ahead is unclear.

My daughter's biological father's tragedy taught me the power of perseverance. Caring for him was one of the hardest things I've ever done, but it also revealed strengths I didn't know I had. I made life-and-death decisions, advocated for his care, and navigated complex emotions. In those moments, I began to see glimpses of my purpose: to be a source of strength and guidance for others navigating their own challenges, whether they were similar to mine or not.

Walking in brilliance also means overcoming lingering doubts and fears. Over the years, I've faced countless moments of self-doubt. Family betrayals, personal losses, and business challenges could have easily derailed me. But each time, I reminded myself of God's promise—that He has a plan for my life, one that is greater than anything I could imagine.

Learning to trust that plan has been a process, but it's brought me to a place where I can celebrate both the big victories and the small, quiet wins.

Living in your purpose doesn't mean life will be free of challenges. It means choosing to rise above them—to keep moving forward even when the road is hard. It means embracing your unique gifts and using them to impact the lives of others. For me, that means sharing my story, mentoring others, and building a business that empowers women to rediscover their brilliance after life's setbacks, realizing that there is life after the pain. The pain was allowed to make us stronger and build our resilience muscles. There is an old saying, " Heavy is the head that wears the crown," but this is much more than just an old saying. Just understanding what this actually means and making it personal makes all the difference in the world. I started to unpack this and examine it and how it shows up in my life. The phrase, *"Heavy is the head that wears the crown,"* originates from Shakespeare's play *Henry IV, Part 2*. It refers to the burden and responsibility that comes with leadership, power, or authority. While many see the crown as a symbol of success and honor, it also represents the weight of decision-making, accountability, and the challenges that come with guiding and protecting others. This is very similar to me and my life's journey. This is what walking out my purpose looks like and feels like.

What It Means to Me Personally:

To me, this saying reflects the reality of walking in purpose and leadership. Wearing the *"Crown"* means stepping into the calling God has placed on my life, even when it feels overwhelming. It's about embracing the responsibility to lead with integrity, strength, and compassion, knowing that the journey is not always easy.

The crown isn't just a symbol of authority—it's a symbol of resilience, sacrifice, and unwavering faith. It reminds me that while the weight may be heavy at times, God's grace sustains me. I wear it not for glory but to serve others, fulfill my assignment, and leave a legacy of impact and empowerment.

The revelation of my daughter's pain—the violation she endured as a child—added another layer to my purpose. It drove me to advocate fiercely for her and others who have faced similar trauma. God turned my anger into a mission, showing me how to channel my energy into creating safe spaces, raising awareness, and empowering survivors to heal and thrive. That experience, as painful as it was, reminded me of the resilience we are capable of when we walk in His light.

If you're ready to walk in your brilliance, I encourage you to take the first step. Trust the process, lean into your faith, and surround yourself with people who believe in you. You are capable of more than you know, and your brilliance is waiting to shine.

Let me remind you again that walking in brilliance requires faith, resilience, and the courage to step boldly into your God-given purpose. It's a journey that evolves over time as we grow through challenges and embrace the lessons life teaches us.

Tips and Tools for Walking in Your Purpose:

1. **Clarify Your Calling:** Spend time in prayer, meditation, or journaling to reflect on what you're passionate about and how it aligns with your gifts.
2. **Take Small Steps:** Don't wait for the perfect moment. Start with small, intentional actions that bring you closer to your goals.

3. **Silence the Doubts:** Write down any limiting beliefs holding you back, then replace them with affirmations that reflect God's promises for your life.
4. **Build a Support System:** Surround yourself with mentors, friends, and leaders who inspire and encourage you to keep moving forward.
5. **Embrace Growth:** Be open to learning from failures and setbacks. Each challenge is an opportunity to strengthen your faith and resilience.

Reflection Exercise: Reflect on a moment in your life when you overcame a significant challenge. Write down how it shaped you and what you learned about your strength and purpose.

"Your brilliance doesn't require permission—step boldly into your purpose."
- Dr. Lashonda Wofford

From Brokenness to Brilliance Focus: Reflecting on the Journey

As I look back on my journey from a 16-year-old mother to a woman walking boldly in her God-given purpose, I am struck by the beauty that has come from the brokenness. Each challenge and each moment of pain has shaped me into the person I am today.

Reflecting on my journey, I see the lessons in every season. Becoming a mother at 16 taught me responsibility and resilience. Being a caregiver to my husband just months into our marriage showed me the depth of love and the power of commitment. Caring for my daughter's father during his final years taught me the importance of advocacy and the strength of the human spirit.

The betrayals and challenges I've faced with family over the past year and a half have been some of the hardest moments of my life. But even in that pain, I've found lessons about boundaries, self-worth, and the importance of standing firm in my truth. These experiences have reminded me that brilliance doesn't come from a life free of pain; it comes from choosing to rise above it.

Discovering my daughter's trauma was a moment that nearly broke me. The guilt, anger, and grief felt insurmountable. But in the darkest moments, I found God's healing power. He took my pain and gave me purpose. He showed me how to use my experiences to uplift others, to create a path of healing not just for my family but for anyone who needed to know they weren't alone. That transformation from brokenness to brilliance is a testament to His grace.

To maintain brilliance amidst life's challenges, I've learned the importance of self-care and faith. Journaling, praying, and moments of quiet reflection have been my anchors. Surrounding myself with supportive relationships and letting go of toxic ones has created space for growth and healing. When the enemy tries to whisper lies, reminding you of your past and convincing you that you are not brilliant, beautiful, or enough, you must stand firm in the truth of who God says you are. Your worth is not defined by your mistakes, failures, or what others say about you—it is rooted in God's unconditional love and His divine purpose for your life. Speak life over yourself when doubt creeps in. Declare that you are fearfully and wonderfully made (Psalm 139:14), chosen and dearly loved (Colossians 3:12), and created for good works (Ephesians 2:10). Do not allow the enemy to dictate your narrative; instead, remind yourself that your story is a testimony of God's power to turn brokenness into brilliance.

Affirming yourself is a powerful act of faith. Speak boldly: "I am a child of God, made in His image. I am more than a conqueror through Him who loves me (Romans 8:37). I am redeemed, forgiven, and set apart for greatness." Repeat these truths daily and let them take root in your heart. Remember, transformation starts from within. Proverbs 18:21 reminds us that life and death are in the power of the tongue, so use your words to align with God's promises. Stand tall in the knowledge that you are enough, not because of what you've done but because of who God is. He has called you by name and equipped you to shine brilliantly despite your past. Your scars are proof of your survival, and your brilliance is a testament to His glory.

Affirmations to Declare Over Yourself:
- I am fearfully and wonderfully made (Psalm 139:14).
- I am more than a conqueror through Christ (Romans 8:37).
- I am chosen, loved, and enough (Colossians 3:12).
- I am created for a purpose and equipped to fulfill it (Ephesians 2:10).
- I am free from condemnation and walk boldly in God's grace (Romans 8:1).

Let your words reflect the truth of who you are, and let your faith in God's promises guide you forward.

Over the years, I've also come to understand the importance of forgiveness. I had to forgive myself for the things I couldn't control, forgive others who caused me pain, and allow God to mend the broken pieces. Forgiveness doesn't mean forgetting—it means choosing to no longer be held captive by the weight of the hurt. I've come to understand that forgiveness is a gift you give yourself. It is not about excusing the behavior of those who have hurt you, minimizing what was done, or pretending that the pain never existed. Forgiveness is defined as the intentional process of releasing feelings of resentment or vengeance toward someone who has harmed you, regardless of whether they deserve it or have asked for your forgiveness. It is not a free pass for their actions, nor does it mean you have to reconcile, re-establish trust, or lower the boundaries that protect your peace and well-being. Forgiveness is a decision you make to free yourself from the emotional prison of bitterness, anger, and hurt so you can live a life filled with peace and purpose.

When I realized that forgiveness wasn't about the people who had wronged me but about my healing, the weight began to lift. Forgiving others doesn't mean allowing them back into your life or leaving yourself vulnerable to further harm—it means letting go of the power they hold over you. Forgiveness is a journey, often messy and imperfect, but it is worth it. Each time I chose to forgive, I found myself lighter, freer, and more open to the blessings God had for me. Holding on to resentment only prolonged my pain, but releasing it allowed God to mend the broken pieces and restore what had been stolen. Forgiving myself was perhaps the hardest but most transformative step. I had to let go of guilt for the things I couldn't control and give myself grace, knowing that God's love and mercy covered my imperfections.

Why Forgiveness Is for You:

- Forgiveness breaks the chains that tie you to the hurt. It allows you to move forward without carrying the emotional baggage of the past.
- Forgiveness restores your peace of mind and emotional well-being, creating space for joy and healing.
- Forgiveness aligns your heart with God's desire for your life. He calls us to forgive, just as He has forgiven us (Ephesians 4:32).

Important Truths About Forgiveness:

- Forgiveness does not excuse the behavior or actions of the person who hurt you.
- Forgiveness does not require reconciliation or trust—those things must be earned and can only happen if the other person is willing to change.
- Forgiveness does not mean forgetting; it means releasing the hold that pain has over you while remembering the lessons that protect your peace.

Reflection Exercise: Take a moment to write down the names of people, including yourself, whom you need to forgive. Then, for each name, write a prayer or statement of release, such as, "I choose to forgive [name] and release the pain they caused me. I will no longer allow this hurt to define my life." End the exercise by writing, "I forgive myself for [specific situations], and I allow God to heal me."

Forgiveness is freedom. It's an act of love toward yourself and a declaration that you will no longer be held captive by the weight of the past. The more I embraced this truth, the easier it became to forgive—not for others, but for me. God's grace taught me that forgiveness is the key to unlocking a life of peace, healing, and brilliance.

If you're on your own journey from brokenness to brilliance, I want to encourage you to keep going. Reflect on how far you've come, celebrate the victories along the way, and don't be afraid to shine your light on others. Your story has the power to inspire and uplift, just as mine has.

Remember, brilliance isn't about perfection. It's about embracing your story, owning your truth and your journey, and using it to make an impact. You are a light in this world, and your brilliance is needed.

I say to you again, looking back on my life, I see how each season of brokenness led to brilliance. It wasn't easy, but every painful chapter has prepared me for the purpose I walk in today.

Tips and Tools for Transforming Brokenness into Brilliance:
1. **Practice Gratitude:** Find one thing each day to be grateful for, even in the midst of pain. Gratitude shifts your perspective and helps you see the beauty in life's challenges.
2. **Prioritize Self-Care:** Healing requires intentional rest. Create a routine that includes prayer, journaling, exercise, and quiet reflection to recharge your spirit.

3. **Seek Professional Help:** Therapy or counseling can provide tools and insights to help you navigate through pain and trauma.
4. **Forgive and Release:** Forgiveness is a powerful tool for healing. Write a letter to yourself or others expressing your feelings and then release the pain through prayer or a symbolic act.
5. **Share Your Story:** Your story has the power to inspire others. Whether it's through writing, speaking, or mentoring, let your journey be a light for someone else.

Reflection Exercise: Write down three lessons you've learned from a difficult season in your life and how they've shaped the person you are today.

FROM BROKENNESS TO BRILLIANCE

ABOUT THE AUTHOR

DR. LASHONDA WOFFORD

Dr. Lashonda Wofford is a dynamic entrepreneur, community advocate, philanthropist and transformational leader. As the founder and driving force behind multiple successful ventures—including L&S Consulting Group, Akins Global Diagnostics Laboratory Solutions and former owner of Akins Helping Hands, a thriving seven-figure home care company based out of North Carolina and now she's added the title of Freelance Writer -----Dr. Wofford has established herself as a powerful force in both business and personal development.

Passionate about empowering others, Dr. Wofford created the "**All Bets on Me**" platform on Facebook, where she inspires individuals to invest in themselves and overcome life's challenges. Her journey, marked by resilience and determination, has led her to achieve numerous goals despite significant adversities. With a PhD in Christian Education, she stands as a beacon of success, particularly for women of color, breaking barriers and paving the way for others to access the same opportunities she has created.

Dr. Wofford's achievements are numerous and impactful. She is an accredited certified instructor and Founder of The All Bets On Me Academy, in partnership with Purpose Zeal Academy and holds certifications as an Executive Leadership Coach, Life Recovery Coach, Mental Health Counselor, and Transformational Coach, Art Therapy Practitioner, Positive Psychology and Trauma Informed Coach (Just to name a few). A prolific author, she is an international ten-time best-selling author with titles including *Blessed Not Broken, Vol. I*; *Igniting Your Purpose*; *90 Days of Biblical Affirmations for Christian*

Women in Business and Ministry; Love Business Marriage; Marketplace Mogul; Girl, Let That Go, her solo work, Pain Equals Purpose, Visionary of Breaking The Chains; Liberating Your Lineage From Generational Curses and Black Diamond Chronicles Vol.1 Her contributions to literature and community service earned her the prestigious 2022 ACHI Award for Public Service. 2023 Author Of The Year from the InspireU Network, 2023 Coach Of The Year from The Power and Grace Leadership Association. Recipient of two Presidential Lifetime Achievement Awards.

Dr. Wofford's demonstration of superior expertise, leadership and professional excellence in her field elevated her to be selected for inclusion in the Nationwide Registries Women of Distinction 2024 Honors Edition. Her solo book Pain Equals Purpose received the 2024 International Impact Book Award in the Autobiography, Female Empowerment, and Inspirational categories. Breaking The Chains; Liberating Your Lineage From Generational Curses was selected and recognized in the highest regards and endorsed by the CEO of the company awarding the book as a winner from christlit Book Awards for the 2024 and 2025 Year. Dr. Wofford has received the 2024 Author of Influence from DWAP (Designed with a purpose) organization and was crowned as Visionary Author of The Year 2024 from the Global Iconic Changemakers of The 21st Century Award form the BPMI Ladies Clubs Global Teas & Birthing Process Ministries International United States of America. Dr. Wofford was also crowned Purpose Driven Person of The Year from the G.B.B. Organization for 2024 and

The Phenomenal Woman Award for 2025 from The Elite Creations Organization.

Deeply rooted in her faith, Dr. Wofford and her husband are active members of Mt. Zion AME Zion Church, where she strives to live out God's plan for her life by serving others. In her personal life, she cherishes time with her family, especially her grandchildren, and prioritizes self-care through relaxation and reading. Residing in North Carolina with her husband and family, Dr. Wofford continues to inspire and lead by example.

Connect with Dr. Lashonda Wofford:

- Website: www.drlashondawofford.com
- Facebook: https://www.facebook.com/lashonda.wofford.7
- All Bets On Me: https://www.facebook.com/share/g/19tkyagDze/
- Instagram: https://www.instagram.com/drlashondawofford/
- All Bets On Me Academy: https://dr-lashonda-wofford-s-school.teachable.com/p/abom

Workbook & Guided Journal

CHAPTER 1:
THE BREAKING POINT
When Everything Changes

REFLECTION QUESTIONS:

Describe a moment in your life that felt like a breaking point. What emotions did you experience?

_____

_____

_____

How did this event change the way you saw yourself and your future?

_____

_____

_____

What were the hardest lessons you learned from this season of life?

_____

_____

_____

JOURNALING PROMPT:

Write a letter to your past self, offering comfort and encouragement during your breaking point. What would you tell yourself now?

CHAPTER 2:
IN THE DEPTHS OF DESPAIR
Coping in the Seasons of Darkness

REFLECTION QUESTIONS:

What are some healthy ways you have coped with dark seasons? What has helped the most?

_____

_____

_____

Have you ever felt lost in your struggles? How did you find your way back?

_____

_____

_____

How has your faith or inner strength played a role in overcoming despair?

_____

_____

_____

JOURNALING PROMPT:

Write about a time you felt completely alone. How did you navigate that pain? What would you say to someone currently in that place?

CHAPTER 3:
FROM BROKENNESS TO BRILLIANCE
Finding Purpose and Passion Beyond Your Pain

REFLECTION QUESTIONS:

How has pain shaped your purpose?

_____

_____

_____

What new strengths or gifts have emerged from your struggles?

_____

_____

_____

If your pain could teach someone else a lesson, what would it be?

_____

_____

_____

JOURNALING PROMPT:

Visualize your future self, walking fully in purpose. Describe what that looks like, how it feels, and what impact you are making.

CHAPTER 4:
BEYOND THE VERDICT
A Journey from Pain to Power

REFLECTION QUESTIONS:

Have you ever felt defined by a situation or label? How did you overcome that?

_____
_____
_____

What does power mean to you in the context of healing?

_____
_____
_____

In what areas of your life do you still need to reclaim power?

_____
_____
_____

JOURNALING PROMPT:

Write a declaration of power: "I am no longer bound by... I am stepping into..."

CHAPTER 5:
TURNING PAIN INTO PURPOSE
Peace Over Panic, Faith Over Fear, Wisdom Over Worry!

REFLECTION QUESTIONS:

How do you choose faith over fear in difficult times?

_____

_____

What practices help you maintain peace when challenges arise?

_____

_____

What wisdom have you gained from your painful experiences?

_____

_____

_____

JOURNALING PROMPT:

Describe a time when you had to make a choice between fear and faith. How did it turn out?

CHAPTER 6:
CULTIVATING PASSION AND CONFIDENCE
Rebuilding Self-Esteem and Rediscovering Joy

REFLECTION QUESTIONS:

What activities or passions bring you joy?

_____

_____

How have you worked on rebuilding your self-esteem?

_____

_____

What are three things you love about yourself today?

_____

_____

_____

JOURNALING PROMPT:

Create a self-love affirmation: "I am worthy of... I deserve... I embrace..."

CHAPTER 7:
FROM SILENCE TO SIGNIFICANCE
Reclaiming My Voice, Boldness, and Brilliance

REFLECTION QUESTIONS:

Have you ever felt silenced? How did you find your voice again?

_____

_____

What does boldness mean to you, and how can you step into it more?

_____

_____

Who or what inspires you to walk in brilliance?

_____

_____

JOURNALING PROMPT:

Write a victory statement: "I will no longer be silent about… because my voice matters."

_____

_____

_____

_____

_____

_____

_____

_____

_____

_____

_____

_____

_____

CHAPTER 8:
FROM BROKENNESS TO BRILLIANCE
The Power of Community and Walking in Purpose

REFLECTION QUESTIONS:

How has community played a role in your healing journey?

_____

_____

_____

Who are the people that uplift and encourage you?

_____

_____

_____

How can you use your story to uplift others?

_____

_____

_____

JOURNALING PROMPT:

Write about a time when someone's support made a difference in your healing journey. How can you be that person for someone else?

CLOSING REFLECTION

As you complete this workbook and journal, take a moment to reflect on your journey.

_____

_____

_____

What is the biggest lesson you've learned about yourself?

_____

_____

_____

What commitments are you making to continue walking in your purpose and brilliance?

_____

_____

_____

_____

FINAL JOURNALING PROMPT:

Write a love letter to your future self, reminding yourself how far you've come and encouraging yourself to keep shining.

"Crowned in Unity"
By Dr. Lashonda Wofford

Through embers and echoes, we rise—
not as solitary flames,
but as a wildfire of purpose,
ignited by grace and bound
by divine design.

We are more than a moment—
We are movement.
A tapestry of soul and strength,
woven with threads of legacy,
drenched in the perfume of resilience.

Sister by sister,
we gather in sacred circles of trust,
where comparison dissolves
and compassion reigns.
Here, healing is not whispered—
it is *declared*.
Love is not lent—it is *lavished*.

We are the balm to one another's bruises,
the echo to silent cries,
the lighthouse in storms

that would dare try to dim
our brilliance beneath their ash.

In our unity, we are invincible—
a symphony of voices
singing purpose back into parched places.
We carry each other—not out of duty,
but out of devotion.

Our crowns are not made of gold,
but of grit, wisdom, and wonder.
We wear them unshaken,
draped in the beauty of becoming,
shining brighter
because of the fire,
not in spite of it.

To every woman who stands—
to every woman who has fallen
and dared to rise again—
you are seen, you are sacred,
and you belong.

Together, we are legacy in motion.
Together, we are light unquenchable.
Together, we are
sisterhood—refined, radiant, and rising.

You are proof that something extraordinary is on the other side of pain. Keep shining, keep believing, and keep walking in your brilliance!

www.ingramcontent.com/pod-product-compliance
Lightning Source LLC
Chambersburg PA
CBHW042258090526
44582CB00005B/107